Women Who Win

Women
Who
Win

by
Francene Sabin

Illustrated with photographs

Random House   New York

For their generosity in giving me so much time and assistance, I would like to thank Lee Greene and Tom Jakab. Thanks also to the many athletes and their coaches who gave me such willing cooperation.

Finally, special thanks to Teddy Slater for her guidance and encouragement.

PHOTOGRAPH CREDITS: Central Press, 13 bottom left; Sam Doherty (Camera 5), 12; Alan R. Ehrlich, 51, 54; London Daily Express, 13 bottom right; Lyn Malone, 15; Professional Women Bowlers Association, 89; Flip Schulke (Black Star), 70, 71; Pamela R. Schuyler, 14; United Press International, half title page, title page, 13 top left, 32, 52, 88, 107, 125, 141, 142, 143, 159 right and left; Wide World Photos, dedication page, 13 top right, 33, 34, 53, 108, 109 top and bottom, 123, 124 top and bottom, 158. Photo on page 35, courtesy of Janet Lynn.

Cover photograph by Dan Baliotti (Movement Associates)

Library of Congress Cataloging in Publication Data

Sabin, Francene. Women who win. Brief biographies emphasizing the athletic achievements of such women as Billie Jean King, Cathy Rigby, Micki King, Cheryl Toussaint, and others. 1. Athletes, Women—United States—Biography—Juvenile literature. [1. Athletes, Women] I. Title. GV697.AlS22 796'.092'2 [920] 74-20835 ISBN 0-394-82832-1 ISBN 0-394-92832-6 (lib. bdg.)

Manufactured in the United States of America 1 2 3 4 5 6 7 8 9 0

To Lou and Keith, whom I love.

Contents

Introduction

Hear the words "sports superstar" and a picture immediately comes to mind. It may be of a major league home-run king, a football quarterback, or a high-scoring basketball player. But whatever image you get, and whatever the sport, it's almost a sure bet the athlete is a man.

The pleasures and rewards of athletics have traditionally been reserved for men. For centuries women were rarely allowed to compete at all, and only in the last 50 or 60 years did it become acceptable for them to do so. But even then, despite the remarkable achievements of a number of female competitors, it was always a "he" who was celebrated nationally and internationally as a superstar.

Never mind that Babe Zaharias was the greatest woman golf and track star in history—the only Babe that every sports fan knew was named Ruth. Never mind that Maureen Connolly and Althea Gibson played tennis well enough to pack the stadiums in the 1950s—for they wore skirts, and that automatically took them out of the superstar category. Debbie Meyer won a hatful of Olympic gold medals in 1968, but after her brief moment of glory, America's greatest female swimmer sank into obscurity.

Yet when Mark Spitz emerged from the '72 Olympics as King of the Pool, he became famous—and rich—overnight.

It's not surprising that girls were rarely encouraged to develop their athletic talents. "Don't bother," was the advice given to most of them. "There's no future in sports for you. Even if you become a champion you won't be able to capitalize on your accomplishments. Who ever heard of a woman making a living in sports?"

Girls were also taught that no normal man would want to date or marry a woman who could outshine him physically. While it was considered natural for boys to be competitive, any girl who was at all serious about sports ran the risk of being considered "unnatural." And if that wasn't enough to turn her off, there were still more dire warnings. Just think of those ugly muscles female athletes develop. Why, look at the bulging biceps of those Russian women. If you run track, your legs will get thick and lumpy. If you swim, your shoulders will get broad and brawny. If you play tennis or golf, the sun will ruin your hair and wrinkle your face. And on and on . . .

But in recent years, attitudes finally began to change. With the emergence of the Women's Liberation movement of the 1970s, females everywhere started to question some of the assumptions that had shaped their lives. In sports, as well as every other field, they challenged financial inequities, demanding equal pay for equal work. At the same time, they began to re-examine some basic sexual stereotypes. Why should physical weakness be thought of as a feminine virtue? What was so unnatural about a woman playing to win? Many females even began to question the traditional standards of "feminine" beauty and wondered how a healthy, well-developed body could be considered anything but beautiful.

As more and more women began to compete, the caliber of their play improved. Before long, it became clear that millions of sports fans (both male and female) found competition between women as exciting as competition between men. And as the most talented women began to emerge as stars in their own right, more and more of their sisters were encouraged to compete.

Exactly who were these pioneers of the 1960s and '70s, these female athletes who paved the way for every young woman who wants to play the game on the same level and with the same opportunities and rewards as men? Who are these *Women Who Win?*

Tennis star Billie Jean King, gymnast Cathy Rigby, figure skater Janet Lynn, and the eleven other athletes introduced in this book are as varied in personality as they are in their physical talents. Yet each is a person with a special will to succeed in her sport. Each was prepared to devote years of endless practice and dedication to a dream of championship. Each was willing to sacrifice the usual pleasures of adolescence to concentrate on her sport. None of them quit when disappointments seemed unbearable and physical challenges unconquerable. None of them took the easy way out by saying, "Well, I'm a girl, so nobody will blame me for dropping out."

Some of them, like Billie Jean King, diver Micki King, and bowler Paula Sperber, didn't even stop when they reached the top. As superstars the equal of any man, they realized it was their responsibility to step forward as spokeswomen for all females who wanted to participate in the world of sport. Not only did they set fine examples of athletic success by their actions, but by speaking out they encouraged young women everywhere to seek the same kind of success.

Becoming a winner is never easy. It takes an incredible amount of talent, determination, and just plain hard work for any fine young athlete to develop into a world-ranked competitor. If the young athlete is a girl, however, it takes even more. Often scorned or ridiculed for her unconventional ambitions, she must overcome not only physical barriers, but emotional ones as well.

How—and why—does a young girl become a champion? What motivates a Micki King to spend long hours, day after day after day, repeatedly climbing up to the platform of a 10-meter diving board, then spinning through space into the water so far below? From that height she knows that one mistake in judgment could mean a shattering collision with the water and the end of her career.

What compels an Olympic track star like Cheryl Toussaint or a champion swimmer like Jenny Bartz to practice to exhaustion, sharpening their starts, building their endurance, ignoring the loneliness and boredom of track and pool? Why do they strive for more speed, better technique, and the sweet satisfaction that comes with victory—victory over the limits of time and space that are called records? For every time a swimmer or runner crouches, waiting for the start of her race, she is not only challenging the clock and other finely tuned athletes, she is challenging herself.

For some athletes, perfection is the name of the game. For others, winning is the only goal. And still others are motivated by the same drives that inspire great generals in combat, business tycoons in industry, explorers of land, sea, and space.

But even with all their talent and dedication, it is doubtful that these athletes could have made it to the top without the help of others. Most often it was a parent who sacrificed the enormous amounts of time and money it takes to develop a champion. Thousands of dollars for lessons and equipment; countless hours of driving to practice, waiting for the session to end before the long drive back home.

Also in the background, but almost as vital as the competitor's talent itself, is her coach. It is the coach who helps mold and condition the raw talent of a promising athlete into matchless championship material. It is the coach who is always on hand to study technique, to offer advice and encouragement, and when necessary to push and to prod.

Coach Fred Thompson guided Cheryl Toussaint to peaks of accomplishment far beyond her expectations, on and off the track. Speaking about the differences between male and female athletes, he said, "Girls seem to get more emotionally involved in track than guys do. I think this is because girls don't have as many athletic outlets. Boys have everything—baseball, basketball, football, school teams of all kinds. If a boy isn't doing well at track, he can walk off and get into something else. For Cheryl and the other girls, this is the only thing they have, and they care. They have tremendous pride in themselves as individuals, and in their team. And competitive? I think girls are much more competitive than boys. Some track coaches may say the opposite, but that's because they've never coached women."

Coaches and parents can only help, however. Ultimately,

winning is up to the individual herself. No amount of guidance from others will make a woman a champion unless she is willing and able to push her mind and body to the extreme limits. That's what separates the winners from all the others.

There can be no doubt that the fourteen women whose stories you are about to read are winners. And through their efforts, a whole new universe is becoming available to all females. The battle they began is not over, however. Equality in sports, as in many other areas of life, is not yet a reality. Most of the best training facilities, funding, coaching, competitive opportunities, scholarships, professional earnings, and public acceptance are still reserved for men. Many fights remain to be fought, and many obstacles must be overcome. But the time is fast approaching when these unbalances will no longer exist. And when that time comes, there are sure to be many more *Women Who Win*.

Women Who Win

Billie Jean King

TENNIS

On September 20, 1973, more than 30,000 people came to the Houston Astrodome to watch 29-year-old Billie Jean King, the world's top-ranked woman tennis player, take on 55-year-old Bobby Riggs, a man who had been a national champion years before Billie Jean was born. The crowd was perhaps the largest live tennis audience ever, and millions of other fans in 37 countries would see the game on television. Billed as the Battle of the Sexes, the match was the most talked-about contest in tennis history.

Billie Jean had already proved that she was the greatest female champion in a generation. She had won the annual singles championship at Wimbledon, England, five times, and in 1971 she had become the first woman athlete in any sport to win $100,000 in prize money in a single year.

On and off the tennis court, Billie Jean had fought for women's rights to equal opportunity in sports. She had been one of the first women tennis players to turn professional—not as a teacher but as a competitor—and had helped establish the first independent women's tennis tour. For years she had carried on an outspoken battle to increase the prize money available to women.

Billie Jean's crusade had won little support from the men who ran international tennis. But her most vocal detractor was Bobby Riggs, former tennis pro, self-proclaimed "male chauvinist pig," and well-known tennis hustler. Riggs had won a name—and a fair amount of money—for himself by challenging people to tennis matches and then betting large sums on himself. To give weaker players a reasonably fair chance against him, he often agreed to play under some rather bizarre handicaps. He had played—and won—a match while holding two large dogs on a leash and had done equally well playing in full woman's attire—high heels and all!

Early in 1973 Bobby proclaimed that women tennis players didn't deserve to win as much money as the men because they didn't play as well. Riggs insisted that women's tennis was a farce and that even he could beat the best female tennis player alive. Then he dared the leading women to play him for $5,000—and the honor of their sex. Billie Jean turned him down flat, but another great champion, Margaret Smith Court of Australia, accepted the challenge.

On Mother's Day, 1973, Riggs and Ms. Court met for a nationally televised best-of-three-sets match. Ms. Court, who had expected to play tough tennis, was totally unprepared for the series of "junk" shots (high-looping lobs and drop-shots) Riggs threw at her. More important, the great publicity build-up for the game—and Riggs' expert needling—had put Ms. Court so on edge that she just fell apart, losing 6–1, 6–2, in less than an hour.

Then the hoopla began. Riggs went around the country proclaiming himself the women's tennis champion and repeating his challenge to Billie Jean, boasting that he could smash her as easily as he had Ms. Court. Billie Jean smiled and waited, certain that the publicity was the best thing that could happen to her and to women's tennis. Then she agreed to play Riggs—but on her own terms. Through husband-manager Larry King, she negotiated with Bobby's representatives for weeks, eventually settling on a $100,000 winner's purse and a share of the television income as well as guarantees for the best playing conditions.

For weeks the match was discussed as the contest between the Libber (Billie Jean) and the Lobber (Riggs). Las Vegas odds-makers favored Riggs heavily, and men all over the world confidently predicted that Billie Jean would fold under the pressure. On and on went the build-up, and up and up went the potential winnings.

Various commercial tie-ins and side bets raised the winner's estimated profit to about $200,000, but there was much more than money at stake. It was beginning to seem as if the whole future of women's tennis was on the line. If the best woman player of the day couldn't even beat a man almost twice her age, how could women hope to be considered equal on the court? The pressure on Billie Jean was almost unbearable.

Finally, the contest took place. The match was played by men's rules, the winner having to take three sets out of five. Using her strong, twisting serve, her phenomenal speed, and her blazing backhand drives, Billie Jean ran Riggs into the ground. She was fast, she was sure, and she was the winner in straight sets (6–4, 6–3, 6–3). After the match was over, Billie Jean flung her racket in the air, wiped away her tears of joy, and said, "I feel this is the culmination of nineteen years of tennis for me."

In a way Billie Jean Moffitt King had spent most of her life preparing for that victory. Born in Long Beach, California, on November 22, 1943, she had been a chubby, active little girl. Her father, Willis J. Moffitt, an engineer with the local fire department, had played basketball and run track in college. He considered sports an important part of every child's life and encouraged Billie Jean and her younger brother, Randy, to be physically active. Every day after school, the two young Moffitts would head for the Houghton Park playground or a nearby beach.

Billie Jean enjoyed football, basketball, track, and softball. "I guess I was a tomboy in those years," she later said, "although I wish there were a better word to describe little girls who happen to like sports."

At the age of ten, Billie Jean was the youngest member of the Houghton Park girls' baseball team. A fast runner and an accurate ball-handler, she was shortstop and lead-off batter. Her fielding and timely hitting helped Houghton Park win the Long Beach Recreation Park Championship—her first sports triumph.

Billie Jean thoroughly enjoyed softball, but it was her brother Randy who eventually became a professional ballplayer. Although the Moffitts were proud of their daughter's athletic ability, they didn't see much of a future for her in baseball. One morning, her father suggested that Billie Jean might be better off trying golf, swimming, or tennis. "I didn't swim well," Billie Jean recalled, "and I considered golf an old man's game. But I always liked to run a lot, so I chose tennis."

At that time, about the only thing eleven-year-old Billie Jean knew about the sport was that it involved running. She actually didn't know what a tennis racket was. And she certainly didn't know the rules of the game. In fact, Billie Jean had never even seen anybody play tennis. Still, she was willing to give it a try.

B.J.—a family nickname that stayed with her from childhood on—played her first game of tennis with a sixth-grade classmate who had been playing for five years. Billie Jean borrowed a racket, and the two eleven-year-olds went out to hit a few. "Of course, I couldn't get the ball back," B.J. said. "After half an hour I told her, 'You aren't getting any fun out of it.' So we stopped, but I was hooked."

To earn money to buy her own racket, Billie Jean did odd jobs around her neighborhood. When she had eight dollars stashed in a glass jar in a kitchen cupboard, she went out to buy her first tennis racket. "It was maroon and had a velvet grip," she remembered. "It had real thick nylon and was loosely strung, factory style. But I was in seventh heaven."

Racket in hand, she went to Houghton Park, where free group tennis lessons were given to neighborhood kids every Tuesday afternoon. It was there, on a cement court, that Billie Jean Moffitt took her first lesson from instructor Clyde Walker.

That day's lesson didn't cover much more than the proper racket grip, but B.J. happily stayed on the court for four hours. When her mother came to pick her up, Billie Jean announced, "Mother, this is what I want for my life. I want to be the best tennis player in the world."

From that day on, tennis became the focus of her life. Clyde Walker coached youngsters at a different Long Beach park every day, and B.J. followed him around as if he were the Pied Piper. She would show up at every session, at every park, ready to learn more. Not surprisingly, Walker noticed the determination of the little girl and began giving her special attention.

Billie Jean played a strong game right from the beginning. She was fast on her feet and, thanks to her shortstop experience, could start and stop, wheel, turn, and cover the court with unusual ease. She played an aggressive game, rushing the net, never letting up for a moment, showing the same drive and desire that would later make her a great champion. The talent was there, the determination was there, and Clyde Walker was there to provide the instruction in the fine points of the game.

Patiently, day after day, he worked on Billie Jean's ground strokes, varying her style of play by tempering her drives to the net with long, smooth baseline moves. Walker knew that Billie Jean needed to develop all the elements of her game if she was to become "the best tennis player in the world."

When she was eleven and a half, B.J. played her first real tennis match against a 16-year-old named Marilyn Hester. B.J. won the first set 6–3 and was ready to leave the court when she was told that the match wasn't over yet. So she kept playing and won the second set 6–4 to wrap it up. "I didn't know you had to play two sets," she explained later. Everyone had assumed she knew that in women's tennis a player must take two sets out of three to win the match.

B.J. continued to work with Clyde Walker, practiced eight hours every day there was no school, and strove to acquire the skills she needed to be a top-notch player. It was far from easy. One of the difficulties was that the fireman's daughter didn't belong to a country club, where most tennis was then played, and was constantly snubbed as the "wrong" kind of person.

Her mother and father weren't at home in the world of tennis either. "As helpful parents they carted me the length and breadth of Southern California to tennis tournaments," Billie Jean explained, "but they always felt out of place and uncomfortable in the club environment I had to compete in. Although they were both sports nuts, it was like pulling teeth to get my parents to tennis matches."

The snobbery and exclusiveness of tennis that B.J. encountered may be hard to imagine today, now that the sport has become so popular. But in 1954 tennis was strictly an upper-class game with very old-fashioned rules of behavior and dress. Back then, colored sneakers were reason enough to get a player thrown off a court. Girls might, if they were very daring, wear a colored belt or hair ribbon, but they weren't permitted to go beyond that limit.

In that rule-bound atmosphere of country club tennis, Billie Jean was an "out," a fact of life she was never allowed to forget. "For my first tournament," she said, "when I was about twelve, Perry T. Jones [then president of the Southern California Tennis Association] pushed me out of the group picture. I was wearing a blouse and a nice pair of white tennis shorts that my mother had made for me. But Jones had this rule: little boys wore shorts and little girls wore dresses, and that was that."

B.J. won her first tournament—the Long Beach Recreation Class D, women's division—when she was 13. The six-inch trophy she received for that victory was the first real sign that her dreams might come true. It still sits in a place of honor today, in the midst of the more impressive international awards Billie Jean later collected.

Life for Billie Jean, aside from tennis, meant Long Beach Polytechnic High School. She was quiet in school, getting good grades but lacking self-confidence. "If I had to give a book report in class," she said, "I was so shy I couldn't open my mouth. I used to get so red. But playing tennis made me meet people, and then I found that if you can just be yourself, it works."

Billie Jean also found time to take piano lessons, and playing the piano gave her a good outlet from the pressures of competition. She played classical and popular music, and years later she would still sit down at the piano whenever the tensions of tennis began to feel overwhelming.

Billie Jean's toughest problems as a teenager were her tendency to gain weight in the off-seasons, and, even more serious, her extreme nearsightedness. At the age of 13 she began to wear glasses on and off the court. Her eyesight was so poor that many experts considered it a miracle that she played tennis at all, and a double miracle that she played so well. Even with the glasses, Billie Jean had trouble seeing. The frames blocked certain areas from vision, creating blind spots on both sides. To make things worse, sweat tended to run down the lenses during a game, and heat caused them to fog over. To combat the fogging of her lenses, Billie Jean learned to rub a smear of soap over each lens just before a match. As she grew accustomed to wearing eyeglasses and solved the problems they caused, her tennis got even better.

When she was 15, B.J.'s court accomplishments were noticed by Joe Bixler, a representative of the Wilson Sporting Goods Company. Mr. Bixler introduced her to America's tennis immortal, Alice Marble, who had been an international star in the late 1930s, winning one Wimbledon title and four U.S. championships.

Ms. Marble watched B.J. in action, recognized the potential in the hard-hitting teenager, and offered to coach her. "I could have fallen over backward—and probably did," said Billie Jean, remembering that moment.

For the next four months Billie Jean spent every weekend in the town of Tarzana, 40 miles from Long Beach. There Ms. Marble gave B.J. countless hours of private lessons, free of charge. Most ranking tennis players learn their game in expensive country clubs and must then pay extra fees for coaching by club professionals, another large expense. Billie Jean was one of the few tennis stars to learn the game on public courts and probably the only one who never paid for a lesson.

Ms. Marble knew that Billie Jean's strength was her aggressive attack at the net and that this phase of her game didn't need very much work. She helped B.J. strengthen her forehand and develop her backcourt ground strokes. "I think she helped me mentally as much as anything else," Billie Jean later said. "More than anything, I think she gave me confidence. She showed me that the more you know about the game, the more confidence you have."

The coaching paid off handsomely. Billie Jean's ranking in U.S. amateur tennis went to 19th in 1960. By 1961, the year she graduated from high school, Billie Jean was ranked fourth. Her plans for the future were divided—to be a tennis star and to do well in college. She intended to get a degree in social studies and then teach at the junior-high or high-school level. "I feel I don't want to go on playing a long time," Billie Jean said at the time.

Billie Jean King rejoices after defeating Bobby Riggs in the "Battle of the Sexes" at the Houston Astrodome in 1974.

Billie Jean shows the form and grace that brought her the Wimbledon trophy in 1967.

In 1974 Billie Jean divided her time, playing team tennis
with the Philadelphia Freedoms (left) and competing
on the Virginia Slims circuit (above).

"There's more to life than just tennis." But that was before she realized just how much the game would change her life.

B.J. enrolled at Los Angeles State College, where she maintained a B average, dated several young men (including classmate Larry King), went to parties, played the piano, danced the twist, ate hot fudge sundaes and then moaned about her weight, and, of course, played tennis.

In 1961 Billie Jean competed in her first Wimbledon tournament. Although she was already well known to American tennis fans, she was a complete unknown on the international scene. When they first saw the 5-foot-6, somewhat plump Californian, the British spectators were less than impressed. B.J.'s behavior on the court—talking to herself, making faces, looking up to heaven in mock despair, sighing, grinning, and frowning—shocked audiences accustomed to the deadpan, upper-class manner of most tennis players. So it was a real surprise when 17-year-old Billie Jean Moffitt and 18-year-old Karen Hantze Susman won the doubles championship, the youngest team in Wimbledon history to do so.

B.J. lost her first match in singles play, but her appetite for the championship was whetted. When asked if she was disappointed by the loss, she answered, "That's all right. I'll come back here and win this little old tournament."

After Wimbledon, everything began to click for Billie Jean. She took the Pennsylvania State Championship, the Philadelphia District Championship, and was named to the U.S. Wightman Cup team. The Cup is awarded annually to the nation that wins that year's U.S.–Great Britain women's competition.

Many tennis buffs didn't believe that B.J. was ready for

Wightman Cup play, but when Darlene Hard and Nancy Richey (the two women who were supposed to be on the U.S. team) were injured before the tournament, the lesser-known players were given a chance. The '61 team was described as the youngest and weakest ever—until B.J. won the singles and doubles matches. The U.S. squad went on to take the Wightman Cup against tremendous odds, recapturing the coveted trophy from the British women, who had held it for three years.

Billie Jean returned to Wimbledon in 1962 ranked fourth among American women. This high status, however, meant little to Wimbledon officials. To them, the fact that she had never won a major singles tournament was far more significant, and they didn't rank her at all. In the opening round of play in the women's singles, Billie Jean was scheduled to face Margaret Smith of Australia, the number one player in the world. It seemed like a sure win for the tall, strong Australian, who was accustomed to winning in top international tournaments.

But B.J. wasn't troubled by the reputation of her opponent. She practiced for the match with a close friend, Carole Caldwell. Carole kept reminding Billie Jean that she had to concentrate on playing to Smith's forehand. In fact, entire practice sessions were devoted to that strategy. As Billie Jean recalled, "Everybody said, 'You can do it, just play her forehand.' But Carole saying it, and repeating it, instilled it in my mind."

On nights before a crucial match, Billie Jean usually had trouble falling asleep, but she slept soundly before this one. And she stepped onto the court with confidence. The first set, which the Australian won 6–1 in only 18 minutes, might have crushed a player with less self-assurance. But Billie Jean wasn't shaken a bit. "As soon as the first set was over," she recalled, "I said, 'Billie, you can do it.' "

In the second set, an aggressive B.J. bounced back to win the first five games. One more game would give her the set and send the match into the third and final set. But then, as Billie Jean recalled, "Margaret started catching up, and I started getting nervous. She started putting in some good shots and I started missing easy ones. It went to 5–3, and then I got over it."

With B.J. ahead 5–3, and needing only one point to win the second set, it was Margaret Smith's turn to be nervous. She hit into the net, and Billie Jean tied the match at one set apiece.

In the final set Ms. Smith took a commanding 4–1 lead. Things looked bad for the young American. As B.J. recalled, "The thought came into my mind, 'At least you've gone three sets.' And then I said to myself, 'That's stupid; you must win this.' "

Using her powerful running backhand, Billie Jean began fighting to catch up. She broke Smith's service, won her own, and began to unnerve the Australian champ. Ripping a steady stream of shots to Ms. Smith's forehand, B.J. successfully worked on her rival's weak spot. When Billie Jean went ahead 6–5, the capacity crowd in the stadium again fell silent. An upset was in the making. But B.J. double-faulted as she tried to drive her serves past her opponent, and the tension increased. Then, with a backhand volley to Margaret Smith's forehand, Billie Jean won the set—and the match. With a whoop of absolute joy, she threw her racket in the air and bounded to the net to shake the hand of her defeated opponent.

In the quarter finals, B.J. was eliminated by Ann Haydon of

Great Britain. Yet even though she hadn't achieved her goal of winning "this little old tournament," Billie Jean Moffitt's performance left no doubt that she was on her way to international tennis stardom. The pluck of the 18-year-old American impressed the fans, and suddenly everyone found charm in B.J.'s nonstop, mid-match self-criticism. Her on-court remarks were repeated everywhere: "That's what I mean about you, Billie Jean—you're just plain dumb" or "Hit the ball, you big chicken" and "Get down, you fat little thing." When she was really upset, Billie Jean would shout, "Peanut butter and jelly!" to the delight of the staid British fans.

After Wimbledon, Billie Jean came home to a slew of problems. The first was a sinus condition that caused severe breathing difficulties. To correct this, she had an operation after the 1963 tennis season. The other physical problem wasn't as easy to remedy. Billie Jean had always been chubby, and now, as she tried to slim down, she found herself feeling sick all the time. It was originally thought that she might have a thyroid condition, which would prevent her from losing weight. When that diagnosis proved false, and Billie Jean continued to feel less than perfectly well, it was suggested that she might have an ulcer.

Her tennis game, after the spectacular win over Margaret Smith, was another problem. Now nothing but winning the most important tournaments would satisfy Billie Jean, and she couldn't seem to do that. She felt torn between school and tennis, convinced that it was impossible to do well in both at the same time. In the winter of 1965, with less than a year left until graduation, B.J. decided it was now or never in her tennis career.

So, with the encouragement of her parents and her fiancé, Larry King, Billie Jean dropped out of college.

"My heart was really in tennis," she said. "I decided to go to Australia for three months and change my game. I had a very weak forehand, and I didn't think my serve was powerful enough. A lot of your power is in just playing—playing all the time. It's timing and rhythm.

"In Australia, the great coach Merv Rose helped me. He changed my forehand and my serve. He taught me all about the game as far as percentage tennis is concerned. That is what the pros use. You have certain patterns. There are certain points that you go for at a given time. Anyway, it was the decision to put my whole life into the sport that took me from number four to number one."

Billie Jean came home from Australia to play in the tournaments on the summer circuit. She reached the finals of the U.S. Nationals, only to lose to Margaret Smith. Still, she finished the season as the second-ranked female player in the United States.

In September 1965 Billie Jean Moffitt married Larry William King. That winter was a busy one for B.J. and Larry. He was finishing college and making plans for law school. She was working hard at tennis. "We can't do much planning for the future," she said then, "and we're definitely not thinking of raising a family yet."

In 1966 Billie Jean won every tournament on the winter circuit, including the U.S. hardcourt and the U.S. indoor singles titles. But those were only preparation for the real thing—Wimbledon.

It was a new Billie Jean who took the court at Wimbledon Stadium in 1966. This time there was quiet on her side of the net. She wasn't going to break her concentration with the chatter that had marked her earlier matches. This time, Billie Jean was playing percentage tennis, using strategy and a game plan against each opponent. This time, Billie Jean was not going to be stopped in the finals.

With her overpowering serve, her speed in sprinting to the net, and her new stronger strokes, Billie Jean King defeated Maria Bueno of Brazil for the 1966 women's crown at Wimbledon.

B.J. had realized part of her dream, but the pressure and tension of winning brought on a recurrence of her old stomach problems. Tests showed that she was suffering not from an ulcer but from an inflamed colon. Late in '66, Larry King explained, "Billie has had increased stomach trouble since last September. It's worse than a simple ulcer—the whole colon is affected. It's also been discovered that she's allergic to milk."

By sticking to a very strict diet of meat, no vegetables (other than occasional hearts of lettuce), and no milk products, Billie Jean soon had her health under control. And in 1967 she won every championship in sight: the U.S. indoor, the Eastern grass court, the U.S. Nationals, and Wimbledon. Naturally, she was awarded the rank of number one woman tennis player in the world.

Her childhood fantasies had come true, but B.J. felt there was still more to do. First, she wanted to make life a little easier for Larry. Billie Jean was still an amateur, and although her expense money helped the couple's strained budget, Larry was working

40 hours a week while taking a full load at law school to help make ends meet. B.J. believed that now it was her turn to earn their keep so that Larry could give up his job. Besides, Billie Jean had a new goal now. "This is a pro-oriented country," she said. "You can't be the best here unless you're a pro."

In the spring of 1968, B.J. signed a pro contract and set to work. Winning Wimbledon for the third straight year, she took her place alongside former tennis greats Maureen Connolly Brinker, Suzanne Lenglen, and Helen Wills Moody, the only others to accomplish that feat.

With Larry as her business agent, B.J. set out on the professional tour. But she quickly discovered that being a female tennis pro, even a superb one, didn't bring in very much money. A man who won a tournament might earn $10,000, but a woman was supposed to be satisfied with $2,000. The women, led by Billie Jean, decided to do something about it. They boycotted the official U.S. Lawn Tennis Association tournaments, publicized the inequities in prize money, and began to organize their own tour. "As the women's player representative," Billie Jean said, "I will attempt to represent the women's position along with what I view to be the best interests of the sport."

Billie Jean's arguments were forceful and articulate, but victory didn't come easily. The same establishment that had snubbed the fireman's daughter years before now resisted these new demands for change. The late 1960s and early '70s were years of turmoil for women, particularly for Billie Jean King. Winning tennis matches and drawing crowds were no longer enough for her; only total acceptance as a pro and equal prize money would do.

In 1971 B.J. won $117,000, followed by $119,000 in 1972. She repeated her Wimbledon victory in '72 and '73, was U.S. champion in '71, '72, and '74, and became the best-known female athlete in history. Still, she had one more dream: to make tennis a popular spectator sport by taking it out of the clubs and putting it into the arenas.

Remembering how Bill and Betty Moffitt had been treated at the country clubs where she had played her first tournaments, Billie Jean said, "People have to feel comfortable at a sporting event. And a lot of people don't think they'd be comfortable at a tennis match. My parents would rather see my brother pitch than me play. [Randy Moffitt was then playing for the San Francisco Giants.] They feel more comfortable among baseball people than among tennis people. People have to be taught that tennis is a very athletic game—that it isn't social."

Billie Jean's success in promoting the joys of tennis could hardly be doubted. In the year after her smashing victory over Bobby Riggs, she became the player-coach of the Philadelphia Freedoms, the most successful team in the new World Team Tennis league. She saw the Virginia Slims tour for women pros (which she had helped start) reach new heights of popularity, and she established a new magazine, *womenSports*, to help carry the message that sports are for both sexes.

She was so busy that it seemed only a matter of time before the game itself would take a back seat to her related interests. But by then, of course, Billie Jean King had already made her point in competitive tennis. She had set the standard against which other women tennis players would measure themselves for years to come.

Janet Lynn
FIGURE SKATING

Almost from the time she learned to walk, Janet Lynn Nowicki could skate. She was born April 6, 1953, in Chicago, Illinois, to pharmacist Florian Nowicki and his wife, Ethelyne. One day when Janet was just two-and-a-half, her parents, pack leaders for her two older brothers' Cub Scout troop, took the boys ice skating. Because they couldn't find a baby-sitter for Janet, the Nowickis brought their toddler along. Mr. Nowicki never forgot Janet's first day on the ice.

"She fell all the time," he recalled, "but she never cried—she always laughed. She never let anyone help her. And before we knew what happened, that little girl had taught herself to skate backward. In no time at all! So we put her in a skating class. Partly that was to help her get over her shyness. She had been in a dance class, but she was so bashful she would sit at her mother's feet and refuse to move around.

"Skating was the thing for her. At three she passed up everybody in the children's class. At three-and-a-half she outskated a class of teenagers. Oh, she was so little then. I remember the skating teacher asked the class to write a report about what they had learned. Janet didn't know how to write, so she brought in a tablet full of crayon drawings."

By the time Janet was four years old, she had outgrown class instruction and was taking private lessons. Even so, there was no one in Chicago with enough training to give her the advanced coaching she needed. Then the Nowickis heard about The Wagon Wheel, a resort in Rockton, Illinois, noted for its fine skating facilities and instructors. There, Slavka Kohout (a former figure skating star herself) could give Janet the advanced coaching she needed.

Janet was still too young to attend school, but she was already a serious student of ice skating. So her parents began driving their four-and-a-half-year-old to The Wagon Wheel Ice Palace, a round trip of 200 miles. "What do you do," her mother wondered, "when all a little girl says is, 'I wanta skate, I wanta skate, I wanta skate'?"

The constant traveling and all the work on the ice was very hard on Janet. Skating was fun, but as soon as she started regular school, her schedule became very complex and time-consuming. The traveling was also getting to be a burden on the Nowickis. If Janet's father did the driving to and from Rockton, he had to neglect his pharmacy. Her mother had two growing boys and a new baby girl to take care of, in addition to Janet, and couldn't give all her attention to one child.

The temporary solution, and one that pleased no one, was to send Janet to live with friends in Beloit, Wisconsin, eleven miles from The Wagon Wheel. This arrangement was a lonely one for the shy child. After a short while, Janet's grandfather, Gust Gerhke, moved to Rockton to give her a home. Janet was happier then, but she still missed her parents, and they missed her, too. Finally, Mr. Nowicki sold his Chicago pharmacy, taking a great financial loss, and the whole family moved to Rockford.

"It was hard," Ethelyne Nowicki said. "He had to start all over again, working in someone else's pharmacy." But the family was together, everyone was happy, and that counted more than anything else.

To keep the other children from becoming jealous of Janet, the Nowickis encouraged them to pursue hobbies of their own. The boys had scouting and wrestling, and younger sister Carol began studying gymnastics. "She hates skating," Janet said of Carol, "because mother was always at the skating rink when I practiced, and Carol got dragged along."

Janet remained the center of the family, however. "You change your whole life," said her mother. "But Janet has talent, we're told. And we love to watch her skate."

Every weekday, Janet would leave Johnson School in Rockford and go straight to the rink for a four-hour practice session with coach Kohout. On weekends and during school vacations, Janet would spend nine or ten hours a day gliding and leaping over the ice.

"In a year and a half," Florian Nowicki said, "I put 26,000 miles on my car just making eleven-mile trips from Rockford to Rockton. So you know how often she skated."

Even in the early years, when there was no way of telling how well she would do in competition, Mr. Nowicki estimated that Janet's annual skating expenses came to about $3,000. Training and performance outfits were incredibly costly. In one year, for example, Janet went through three pairs of custom-built skates at $150 a pair. "We hope to keep it up as long as our money holds out," Mr. Nowicki said. "Her goal is to reach the top in amateur status. You get no money from this . . . but this is what she wants."

Janet entered her first big skating competition when she was seven. On her coach's advice, she dropped her last name for the event. "Nobody could ever pronounce it right," Janet explained. And Slavka Kohout added, "It was such a hard name for announcers and the press to get right. I suggested it would be wise, in the interests of simplicity, to drop or shorten the name of Nowicki. Her mother said we could use her first and middle names. She was such a petite, graceful little thing to be hauling around a big name like Nowicki."

It was clear to Janet's coach from the beginning that Janet had the potential to be a champion. "There are people who are winners instinctively," Ms. Kohout said, "and I think Janet showed that even when she was a little, little girl. I think now that perhaps I started her too early in serious competition, but she was that good! She had an animal grace. She had a sense of balance that was incredible, something innate that cannot be taught. And she had character. I have never seen anyone with the drive of Janet. She had the two things no coach can put into a skater—superb balance and strong character."

It took only two years for Janet Lynn to reach the Nationals, for which she qualified by taking third place overall in the Midwest Championships in 1963. Even then, the strengths and weaknesses that were to mark Janet's later career showed clearly. At the Midwest meet, competing in the Novice class, nine-year-old Janet took second place in free skating, the beautifully choreographed routines that counted for 40 percent of the total score. However, she placed only third in the compulsory school figures that made up the other 60 percent. From the outset, Janet had trouble maintaining the concentration and precision needed for school figures—the painstaking, repetitive tracings on the ice of a perfect circle, a figure eight, a double three.

But Janet's free skating was brilliant, lyrical, and majestic. Firmly in the tradition of American figure skating (and figure skating was originally American), Janet's free skating was ballet on ice. "Her strong points are jumping and spinning," said Ms. Kohout. "And she's terrific in free skating. Right now she does the second most difficult jump for figure skaters, the double axle, which consists of a jump and three revolutions in the air. Only about one percent of figure skaters today use the double axle."

Janet was the youngest entrant at the '63 Nationals in Long Beach, California—and the youngest ever to qualify. All the other skaters in the Novice events were teenagers, experienced in high-level competition. But nine-year-old Janet was new to the whole thing—the pressures, the crowds, the intense rivalries. She was so small, so young. Nevertheless, she put on a dazzling show. Although she failed to win any prizes, she did win the heart of everyone who watched her skate.

The magic was there; the only things missing were experience and discipline, the essential ingredients of a perfect performance. After the Nationals, Janet returned to The Wagon Wheel to work some more. Any day, every day, she could be seen gliding across the silvery ice. Like a bird in flight, she soared through her free-skating routines. Only when she faced the demands of school figures did she look earthbound. Then, her mouth grimly set and her forehead lined with concentration, she strove to follow the exacting geometric patterns that seemed so dull and endless.

The Rockford school system bent attendance rules to let Janet skip hours and even days of classes as long as she maintained her grades. Spending hour after hour at the rink—before and after school—left little time for all the other activities she enjoyed. Football games, youth group meetings, and just plain fun had to be carefully squeezed into her already overloaded schedule. Although she was totally dedicated to her time-consuming sport, Janet made every effort to live a normal life.

Janet's close friends accepted her intense desire to skate, but many of her classmates were less tolerant. "I'd come into school after practicing all day," she recalled," and I'd have greasy hair and look really messy. I knew the kids were saying, 'That girl's really crazy.' I worried about it, but not too much. Skating was something I loved to do so much that I wouldn't stop just because someone at school made a funny face. Anyway, the people who were my real friends understood."

There was understanding at home, too. Duty, discipline, and achievement were values the Nowickis instilled in their children. Janet's older brothers were now away at college, where both were excellent students and varsity wrestlers. Little Carol was a fine competitive gymnast, and both parents were hard-working, devout churchgoers. The whole family encouraged Janet as she pursued her difficult course.

In 1966, at the age of twelve, Janet won the Junior Figure Skating Nationals. The 1968 Olympics were only two years away. She hoped to be chosen for the U.S. team, but time was short and there was still so much to learn. The circle of Janet's life was the cold, lonely ice rink. She would attend school for about half the year, then go to summer school to make up what she had missed. She did what was required in the classroom, but her greatest efforts were reserved for the skating rink.

"I spend four to ten hours a day on the ice, six days a week," Janet explained. "It's a necessity. If I don't skate for a week or two, the ice feels foreign to me. You have to get into it, get to feel that it's part of you."

In January 1968 Janet took top honors in the Midwest Figure Skating Championships, qualifying for the Nationals to be held later in the month. This was an important win for her because it was in the Senior rather than the Junior division. She was in the big time now. The three highest-scoring seniors at the Nationals would go to the Olympics. Peggy Fleming, U.S. champion since 1964, was sure to make the squad, which left two other spots open. Janet prayed that she might get one of them.

Janet performed brilliantly at the Nationals. The audience was captivated by the grace and lightness of her leaps and spins in the free skating. As expected, her school figures were still far from perfect, but the thousands of hours of practice had helped. With her free-skating exhibition receiving an almost perfect score, Janet clinched the third place on the Olympic team, behind Peggy Fleming and Albertina Noyes.

That year, 1968, belonged to Peggy Fleming, who swept the National, Olympic, and World Championship titles. But it was also a big year for Janet Lynn. The 14-year-old put on an Olympic show at Grenoble, France, that stamped her as the heiress apparent to her countrywoman and teammate. She was the youngest skater ever to make the U.S. Olympic skating team and an unknown to world competition; but the tiny 5-foot-1 American cast a spell over the crowd with her beautiful free skating. Still, her weak school figures cost her a medal. Finishing a respectable ninth in the Olympics, Janet went on to the World Championships, where she again placed ninth. Being the ninth-best skater in the world was no small achievement, but Janet wasn't about to settle for that.

When Peggy Fleming turned professional after the Olympics, every skater in America began vying for her title. Among them was Janet Lynn, who worked feverishly to perfect her routines. She spent countless hours shaping and developing new and more daring free-skating combinations to perform at the 1969 Nationals.

First on the program were the compulsories, which a nervous Janet skated badly. When she entered the arena for the free skating, it seemed that only a miracle could carry her to the championship. Perhaps the miracle (and that's exactly what Janet thought it was) did take place, or perhaps it was her flawless triple jump (a trick never before attempted in women's competition). She stunned the fans and judges with a come-from-behind four minutes of matchless free skating to win her first Nationals championship.

It was about then that Janet, a devout Lutheran, began to wonder what force was behind her skating. She felt certain that, alone, she could never have gotten so far. Janet said, "When I try to do things for my own satisfaction, I'm never satisfied. When I try to find satisfaction in material things, I'm never satisfied. I have a feeling that God has made me and He knows me better than anyone. He can guide me into what's best for me."

Janet Lynn smiles at the crowd after a 1973 performance (left). A twelve-year-old sensation in 1966 (below), she whirls through her free-skating routine at the Junior U.S. Nationals.

In 1972 Janet traces her compulsory
figures with grim concentration
(left), but glides joyously through
a free-skating routine.

Janet prayed every day, on and off the ice, for guidance, for strength to carry on the long, tedious practices, for faith in herself and in others, and for an end to fear.

"Janet is skating on two thin blades and with a heart full of fear," Ms. Kohout said. "For a figure skater there is fear of falling, fear of failing, fear of the audience. When I think of the discipline, the muscular control, the emotional stresses, the athletic demands in this sport, I wonder that anyone could do it."

With prayer, faith, and work, Janet did it. Although the world title kept going to European skaters, who were more precise in school figures, it was Janet who thrilled the fans with her sensational free skating. At the 1970 World Championships in Ljubljana, Yugoslavia, Janet's performance was hailed by one Olympic skating coach as "the epitome of skating." Still, hampered again by her weak compulsories, Janet finished sixth overall.

She tried to be philosophical about her setbacks, yet there were times when she felt very discouraged. On those gloomy days, when all the work and all the prayers failed to raise her spirits, Janet would sulk and overeat. Then she realized she had a weight problem, a serious handicap for a skater. She looked attractive when she was plump, but every extra pound affected her balance. Applying her usual stoic determination, Janet put herself on a strict diet—and stuck to it.

Off the ice, life continued as before. A full-time student at Guilford High School in Rockford, Janet spent most of her "spare" time skating and sleeping. There was little opportunity to do anything else. "There were times in junior high school and high school when I used to get envious of other girls my age," she said. "I wished I could go to football games and dances. Of course, when I practiced seven hours on the ice, I couldn't think of football and dances.

"When I'm home, it's difficult for my friends to realize why I don't want to talk on the phone or want anybody to come over. But I'm so tired, I just want to go to bed. I've been competing since I was seven years old. It's been a lot of hard work. There have been some depressing times and occasions when I would lose motivation and want to call it quits."

But Janet didn't call it quits. By 1971 she was ranked number one in the United States and fourth in the world. She had graduated from high school and was free to give every moment and every bit of her energy to skating.

Straining for perfection on 5/32 of an inch of steel blade was exacting and torturous. Over and over and over, Janet toiled at her school figures, aiming for geometric precision. Pierre Brunet, a great coach and former gold medal skater, guided Janet in every phase of her figure work. He was patient, gentle, and persistent.

"I do not think there is any other sport so difficult as figure skating," Mr. Brunet said. "Average human beings cannot do it. It uses the whole body. It requires equilibrium; it requires a perfect ambidexterity. No other sport requires such ambidextrous performance as figure skating.

"You have to be able to spin like a top without falling and yet be athletic enough to jump like a gazelle and land on one foot—either foot—and not fall. You must have tight and precise control to draw the figures—the circle does not lie—and you must have the ability to skate like a ballet dancer to great music. You have only one chance before an audience. You must be perfect in all this or you fail. There is no sport that demands so much of a performer as figure skating."

Janet's skating in 1971 was so breathtaking that the spectators booed the judges at the World Championships when they ranked her fourth. Again, the international scoring system that stressed mechanical exactitude over grace and creativity, worked against her. Nevertheless, those were the rules, and Janet simply had to accept them and sharpen herself for the Olympics.

Janet felt ready for anything in Sapporo, Japan, at the 1972 Winter Olympics. Sixteen years of skating and approximately $100,000 invested in lessons, equipment, costumes, traveling, and entry fees had been devoted to this moment. So had a family's dream and an 18-year-old's prayers and sacrifices.

But in Sapporo, the ghost of performances past continued to haunt Janet. She towered above all rivals in the free skating—but again failed to meet the measure of world standards in the school figures. Janet was awarded the bronze medal, finishing behind Beatrix Schuba of Austria and Karen Magnussen of Canada.

Burying her disappointment, Janet went on to the World Championships, where she repeated her Olympic performance and took another bronze. Then she left for home, tired and let down after all the excitement.

Once more, as in the past, Janet turned to God. A member of the Fellowship of Christian Athletes, she took off on a world evangelical tour to tell others how the Bible influenced her life. She spoke of the troubles of holding onto her "real self," and of the ways in which faith and prayer had supported her. "My ego would go flying," Janet said, "and I'd have to control it. You start thinking about material things, about extravagance and being on a pedestal, and then you have to stop and realize—that's not me, that's someone else's idea of me."

Home from the tour, Janet talked about ending her competitive career. Her family and coaches urged her to continue skating, reminding her that the 1973 competitions were drawing closer and it was time to start practicing. Still, she hesitated.

Then, one day, she was back on the ice again. "My being here now," Janet said, "is only because of God. I didn't want to skate this year. I couldn't face it, I was tired. After the Olympics I was sick of it. I was bored and depressed. I almost quit for good this summer. One day I went to the rink. I was planning to work five or six hours. I stayed ten minutes and went home and said, 'Mom, I can't do it.' I talked to my parents, my brothers, and my pastor. I prayed to God about it. He said, 'Skate another year for me.' I said, 'Okay, Lord, if You want me to skate, I will. But then I have to trust You every day because I am tired of it.' He promised, so I am here. But it is so hard and I am more depressed than I was before. I'm okay when I trust in God, but otherwise not. It's so hard now."

As difficult as the endless practicing had become, Janet found the strength to stick with it—particularly the school figures. Pierre Brunet said, "Janet's problem is lack of concentration. You cannot let go for one split second. You cannot think of one thing else when you are doing figures. It is a matter of perspective and balance. Some people have a gift for drawing circles, others do not. To do figures well you must concentrate only on figures for three hours a day, every day. A juggler does not learn to balance a plate on his head and toss a spoon into it without full concentration and full days of practice. I've seen some improvement in Janet's concentration. But whatever happens, remember —the circle doesn't lie."

Janet struggled for concentration and control, but sometimes they eluded her. To bubble and leap and dance—that was her way. She took first place in the 1973 Nationals, her fifth straight win there. But she still hadn't captured an international title, and the '73 World Championships would be her last chance to win one. Win or lose, Janet planned to retire after that competition.

She would have a better chance this time, because the scoring system that always worked against her had finally been changed. School figures now counted for only 40 percent of the total, not 60. The four-minute free skating was still worth 40 percent, and a new, compulsory two-minute free-skating program made up the remaining 20 percent. So Janet went off to Bratislava, Czechoslovakia, and fans the world over waited to see if she would finally go all the way to the top.

The glides and leaps, the pirouettes and turns were stupendous, but the championship was not to be hers. To the disappointment of the spectators, who cried with the frustrated American, Janet messed up her compulsory figures and had to be content with the silver medal. Canada's Karen Magnussen claimed the first-place trophy.

Janet found comfort in the belief that it was God's will. "This year at the World's," she said, "I fell down twice. At first it hurt me that I hadn't done as well as I had hoped, but now I realize that it was what God wanted for me. He wanted people to know that I was human and that I make mistakes."

This time, when Janet returned to Illinois, she was content even though she hadn't won. She was soothed by the knowledge that she had always given her all, and that she had earned a rest. And the first thing she wanted to do, Janet said, was "to get off my diet and eat a gallon of ice cream." That major task completed, she looked around to see what else life had to offer.

For several years, ice-show promoters had been making tentative offers for Janet to turn professional. But it had been too soon. Now the time was right and, with former U.S. Olympic ice skating champion Dick Button guiding her career, 20-year-old Janet agreed to appear with the Ice Follies. She signed a contract for $1,422,000—the largest amount ever paid to a female athlete. It wasn't only the money (much of which Janet immediately donated to charity) that delighted her. Now, at last, she would have the opportunity to do the unshackled, beautiful skating she loved, without the drudgery of those tiresome circles.

"When I decided to turn professional, I knew the pressure would be less," Janet said. "But even more, I didn't think God wanted me to skate another year for the gold medal. I possibly wouldn't have gotten it anyway.

"Before, I was always fighting the bit about competing against someone. I was tired of competing, but I wanted to use my ability. I just didn't want to skate to beat someone else. I wanted to skate for the love of it. Now I'm sharing what I'm doing with an audience, and it's more relaxed. I don't feel I have to do everything perfectly."

And then, perhaps because she didn't *have* to, Janet competed again. Only this time the rules were different, and she was matching her skills against those of other pros. The First Professional Figure Skating Championship took place in January 1974. When it was over, none other than Janet Lynn skated into the spotlight to finally receive the applause reserved for number one.

She bowed and flashed her familiar, sweet smile. The years of travel and competition had matured her, and the once-shy girl had become a warm, confident woman. From that day on she was poised in interviews, comfortable with herself and others, happy to be doing the kind of skating she had always loved.

Performing her solo act, she looked like some wild, liberated fairy-tale creature. Audiences were awed by the sight of the graceful skater spinning, leaping, and dancing across the glittering ice. But Janet and those close to her knew that her seemingly effortless grace was the product of years and years of sheer determination and hard work in what may well be the world's most difficult sport.

Cheryl Toussaint
TRACK

In 1967 a city-sponsored group called Youth in Action held a track meet at the Boys' High School field in Brooklyn, New York. Because she had nothing better to do that day, 13-year-old Cheryl Toussaint went to watch the meet. Sitting in the stands with her friends, Cheryl found it all very exciting: the speed of the sprinting girls, the yells and cheers of the spectators, the highly charged atmosphere of noise, tension, and fun.

While the meet officials were arranging the order of final events, an "open" race for girls was announced. That meant that any girl present could come to the starting line and compete even if she didn't belong to a track team. Cheryl loved to run—on the street, in the schoolyard, or in the local playground —and she wanted to enter. Still, she hesitated. The girls she had been watching in the meet looked so fast. Cheryl's friends urged her to give it a try. "Go ahead, don't be chicken," they teased. And when one said, "I dare you," Cheryl accepted the challenge.

She was wearing a dress and a pair of sandals, hardly suitable clothing for a race, so a friend who was wearing sneakers swapped footgear with Cheryl. Of course, the fit wasn't exactly right, but it was the best available. Then another girl, who had

43

changed into track shorts, lent her jeans to Cheryl. "Suited up" this way, Cheryl walked down to the starting line and waited for the race to begin.

"It was a hundred-yard dash," Cheryl remembered, "and I really didn't know what to do. I didn't even know how long a hundred yards was. I just stood at the line in someone's dungarees and someone else's sneakers. I didn't know how to start; I was standing straight up. Then the man said, 'Take your marks . . . Set . . . Go!' and I ran. I got second."

There were several qualifying heats being run, and Cheryl was told that the finals would be held in awhile. As she waited, Cheryl began to wonder whether she should enter the finals. "For some reason, I began to hurt right around my hip area, and I didn't understand it. So, I told my friends that I didn't think I'd run. They began the teasing routine again, saying that I was chicken and that I was copping out because I didn't think I was going to win, and that kind of thing. Well, that did it. I went back on the track, ran the final, and took fourth place. That wasn't bad, but the thing that got me was that the three girls ahead of me were all Atoms. I was so impressed with how fast they were that all I could think of was how I could join the team, too."

The Atoms Track Club of Brooklyn was an AAU (Amateur Athletic Union) team, made up of local girls who wanted to run competitively. There were many fine runners in the group, and it was beginning to develop into a real track power.

After the meet was over, Cheryl saw some Atoms runners doing exercises on the grass. Screwing up her courage, she walked over to them and asked how she could join the team.

44

They told her that joining was easy: all she had to do was come to the practices every afternoon.

For a while, Cheryl went to Prospect Park in Brooklyn for the Atoms' daily practice. But when no one paid much attention to her, she began to doubt herself and the results of her running. "I thought that because I was putting my whole heart into it, the coach should have done more than tell me to run laps, do exercises, or practice starts," she said.

Cheryl had no way of knowing that Atoms coach Fred Thompson always treated new team members this way. It was his way of testing their willingness to work. Realizing that the tough, time-consuming practice sessions were more than many girls would endure, he would watch them without their being aware of it. Then, if they stayed with it without any encouragement, he would be sure that they were ready for real coaching.

After two months as an Atom, Cheryl dropped out of the club. The memory of her one race, however, kept coming back to her—the pounding heart before the start, the wonderfully free feeling of running, the excitement of coming in ahead of others. So after six months away from the Atoms, Cheryl Toussaint returned to the club, this time to stay.

Those six months away from track had given the teenager time to think about herself, her attitude toward work, and her goals in life. Cheryl decided that she really cared about track, and she went out to the Prospect Park field ready to dig in and work, even if *nobody* paid any attention to her or praised her.

Fred Thompson had missed Cheryl during those six months, and had hoped she'd come back. He had sent a message to Cheryl, telling her she'd always be welcome. The coach hadn't pressed the issue, but he was very pleased when she did return.

The season for cross-country racing (long-distance races over all kinds of terrain) was just beginning, and Fred took the Atoms to a cross-country meet on Long Island, New York. That day Cheryl officially competed for the first time as an Atom, and neither she nor the coach ever forgot it.

"Cheryl had been back training with us for only about two weeks," Thompson recalled, "but I decided to enter her in a one-mile run, just to give her some competitive experience. Of course, she wasn't really in condition, and I knew it. So, I said to her before the race, 'Don't go out too fast, stay with the pack, and just try to finish.'

"Well, the gun went off, and before I knew it, Cheryl was a hundred yards in front of the whole field and running like a madwoman. I said to myself, 'My gosh, this kid is going to pass out!' But she just kept running. Then, with about a hundred yards to go, the oxygen debt really hit her, and she just about collapsed. She fell down, then got up and started crawling on her hands and knees. It was unbelievable! She stood up, staggered some more, got about twenty yards from the finish line and fell again. She kept on going, crawling, still with nobody near her, and then right at the wire another girl caught up and won.

"Cheryl cried like a baby. I went over and picked her up, tried to comfort her, telling her that she had nothing to be ashamed of. But she just cried. I knew, at that moment, that this girl was going to be something special. I had never seen anything like that before in my whole life."

Until Fred Thompson came into her life, nobody had ever thought of Cheryl Toussaint as something special. Shortly after

Cheryl's birth on December 16, 1952, her parents separated and Cheryl went to live with her grandmother. Her home was a tenement flat in Bedford-Stuyvesant, Brooklyn, one of the worst slums in the United States. In the crowded ghetto schools she attended, Cheryl slipped further and further behind grade level until, by junior high, she was classified as a "slow learner." It was humiliating to be placed in Corrective Reading and Corrective Math, to be kept out of regular classes, and to be forbidden to take the courses that would make her eligible for a good academic high school.

Then Cheryl joined the Atoms, and everything in her world, including school, took on new meaning. Fred Thompson assumed the role of the father she lacked at home, demanding that Cheryl do better, scolding her when she let up, praising her when she succeeded. "Freddy always encouraged me and all the girls to try for good grades," Cheryl explained. "He'd say, 'When those report cards come in, I want to see them!' and he really meant it. He made me feel that he was just as concerned with how I was doing in school as with my running. It was almost as if he were a parent—only having had so much education himself, he really knew what was going on. I couldn't tell him that a C was okay because the teacher had said so—he knew better. My mother and grandmother cared, and were concerned about my schooling, but Freddy knew what each grade meant. There was no snowing him."

With new motivation, Cheryl set to work. She begged the school authorities to let her take algebra, a foreign language, and more advanced English courses. The teachers seemed certain that Cheryl wouldn't be able to do the work, but she was insistent.

Finally, they agreed to let her carry those subjects, in addition to her remedial classes, on a one-year trial. It was grueling, but Cheryl gave it everything she had, and began to learn and do well.

"When I got my report card," Cheryl said, "not only did I feel good for myself in getting good grades, I felt proud having somebody else to show them to, somebody who really appreciated them. Freddy would say, 'Cheryl, that's darn good. Keep it up.' Then he started to talk about college."

Few Bedford-Stuyvesant youngsters go to college, and many don't even finish high school. So to Cheryl, Fred Thompson's mention of college sounded like a wild fairy tale. But she understood, as did all the Atoms, that Fred meant every word he said. He told them that if they were good enough, poverty would never stop them. For example, if they qualified for the Nationals, no matter where the competition was held, he'd see that they got there. An attorney at New York's Madison Square Garden, he would use his own salary, or borrow the money, or beg for it—but the Atoms never had to worry about how they would pay for track equipment, travel expenses, or entry fees.

Her part of the bargain, Cheryl learned, was to succeed in school (flunk and you were off the team) and to work doggedly on the track. And she stuck with the hard, two-hour practice every day. "When I first joined the team," Cheryl remembered, "it was plain exhausting. I'd come home after practice barely able to shower and eat; all I wanted to do was sleep. My grandmother was accustomed to the energetic, bouncy kid I had been, and here I was—collapsing.

"Even though it knocked me out, the running definitely

helped me do better in school. I had to be very well scheduled. If I hadn't been running track every day, I'd have been at the nearest park, playing handball or softball, after school. But with those early-evening practices being so tiring, I knew I had to devote afternoons to homework if I wanted to graduate."

As her schoolwork improved, so did Cheryl's performance on the track. She loved the feeling of running and now, with coach Thompson's faith in her and her own new image of herself, she began turning in faster times and winning races. Cheryl had been running for only about a year when she qualified to compete in the U.S. trials for a place on the 1968 Olympic squad.

Looking back at that time, Cheryl later said, "I had been doing fairly well, but at that point I didn't think I was ready for the Olympics. It was enough of a thrill to know that I had made it to the trials. In a way, it was scary for me. I ran and did the best I could, coming in fifth, but I didn't make the Olympic team. I was a little disappointed, but I know now that if I had qualified for the team then, it might have been the ruination of me. Athletes can be thrown, and I've seen it happen to some when they advanced further than their emotional levels could cope with. Success too soon isn't always a good thing. Sometimes people aren't mentally ready for things, and I think I wasn't ready for the Olympics then."

Cheryl was ready to become an outstanding student, however. Fred Thompson had convinced her that she was college material and that with a little more effort she might earn a scholarship. With that goal firing her up even more, the "slow learner" was soon getting A's and zooming to the top of her class.

In June 1970 Cheryl graduated from Erasmus Hall High

School in Brooklyn and received an academic scholarship to New York University.

"It might sound kind of boring," Cheryl said of her teen years, "because my life was a round of sleeping, eating, classes, running, studying, and more sleeping. But I was doing what I loved and what I wanted to do, and, anyway, there were those marvelous trips every year."

As one of America's top-ranked runners, Cheryl traveled to meets throughout the United States and Europe. The overseas trips gave her an opportunity to measure herself against foreign competition. Best of all, they gave her a chance to see new places, meet people from other countries, and learn through new experiences.

Running took Cheryl to Europe many times and to the U.S. Nationals year after year. Each trip was fun and each was a challenge, but they were only preparation for Cheryl's highest athletic priority—the Olympics.

The teenage runner made the Games the focus of her entire life, even to the extent of minoring in German at college so she would be able to communicate in Munich in 1972. Only two things mattered—school and track. Being so dedicated didn't leave much free time for dating. While Cheryl went out with boys occasionally, she felt it was wrong to establish a serious relationship while she was in training.

"There was one boy," she said, "with whom I went to high school, and I saw him for about two years. But then, I was always so busy that I finally felt it wasn't fair to him or me. To go steady, I'd want to devote time to him, which would have meant taking time away from something else I'd like to do. So it

Cheryl (far left) is just behind the leaders as she makes her move during the 800-meter event at the 1971 U.S. Invitational Track Meet. At right, she crosses the finish line in first place.

Younger teammates eagerly reach out to Cheryl during an Atoms practice session in Brooklyn, New York.

just got to be a hassle. I had many male friends, but on a casual basis. When I wanted to go out, I'd call a friend and suggest something, and I'd feel free to say yes or no if someone called me. I liked it that way because I wasn't misleading anyone."

Although she had a less active social life than many girls, Cheryl did not feel insecure about it—most of the time. She did, however, remember a time when it bothered her a lot. "I was about sixteen," she explained, "and going through a stage when I was always moaning that I wasn't going out enough, and that I always had to call off my dates. Looking back, I think I just couldn't differentiate between the important and the unimportant. Fortunately, I outgrew that!"

Fred Thompson encouraged Cheryl and all the Atoms to lead sensible, well-regulated lives and to take good care of their health. Cheryl always needed a lot of sleep and made sure she got enough. Weight was never a problem for her, as she naturally tended to be thin, but she tried to stick to solid foods and avoid sweets and excess starches.

"My only advice to Cheryl," Thompson said, "was to drink plenty of orange juice and stay with Grandma's food. That was what made her a healthy kid in the first place. Of course, when she was living in a college dormitory, Cheryl had to take care of herself. But by that time, she knew that the wrong foods or a lack of sleep would show in her running. She was too highly motivated to let that happen, so I never had to worry about her."

Cheryl's only recurring health problem was menstrual cramps. Every female athlete must learn to deal with her monthly cycle and not let it interfere with her sports performance. Fred Thompson reminded his runners that menstruation is a normal body function and that it need not prevent a girl from working out or competing. The Atoms were expected to run all month, and Cheryl always abided by that rule. Sometimes she felt terribly uncomfortable before a meet, and just as uncomfortable after, but while she ran she forgot the discomfort and did her best.

Cheryl's sights were set on the 1972 Olympic team, and nothing was more important than that. Every meet counted, because every race was a rehearsal for the big one. During the indoor season in the winter of 1971–72, she was undefeated. She won the 440-yard dash at the Millrose Games, the 880-yard runs at the Maple Leaf Games in Canada and at the AAU Indoor Track and Field Championships, and the 800-meter run at the Olympic Invitational Track Meet. She was faster every time out, and everything seemed to be falling into place.

Then the outdoor season began, and Cheryl had to run a time outdoors that would qualify her for the U.S. Olympic team. She began to press, and lost her concentration on the track. Coach Thompson tried to calm her, to reassure her that a good running time depended on good competition, and that she would make the team. Soon she had qualified as a runner on the metric mile relay team. But she still hadn't qualified in her individual event, the 800 meters. And the summer was growing short.

Fred took Cheryl to Ohio, where there were to be two meets that would give her the opportunity to qualify. On the day of the first meet, Madeline Manning Jackson, the one woman who might have challenged Cheryl and made her run a fast time, came down ill. With nobody challenging her, Cheryl won the race, but her time still wasn't fast enough. At the second meet, Thompson was depending on Nancy Shafer, another top

American runner, to push Cheryl to go all-out. But in the 95-degree heat on the day of the race, Nancy faded away, and from the first turn, Cheryl ran alone. Again she missed running a qualifying time.

Cheryl went to the Olympic training camp with just one last chance to make the team in an individual event. "On the day of the race," Fred Thompson recounted, "I sneaked in, so that Cheryl wouldn't see me. I hid behind a tree and watched her run. When she had done it, qualifying, I came out and she saw me. Well, we both cried and cried in relief. It was really down to the wire on that one."

Then she was off to Munich and the 1972 Olympics. Her first event was the 800-meter run, her specialty. In the qualifying heat, she followed Fred Thompson's advice never to fall farther back than third—with disastrous results. She failed to qualify and was out of competition for the medals. "If she'd been in any other heat, my instructions would have been fine," Mr. Thompson said afterward. "But the girls in her heat went out so fast that Cheryl was thrown off her normal pace and didn't make it. It was my mistake, and I'll never stop blaming myself. If Cheryl had run her usual race, pacing her first quarter more slowly, she'd have made it to the semifinals and then, maybe, to the finals."

The night after the race, Thompson went looking for Cheryl in Olympic Village and found her in tears, broken-hearted at what she considered her failure. Fred consoled her, reminding her that she was the youngest one in the event, that her running career was just beginning, and that there would be another Olympics for her. Besides, the relay race was yet to come. Cheryl still had one more chance to win a medal.

On September 9, 1972, the first women's 4 × 400-meter relay in Olympic history was set to be run. The U.S. team of Mabel Ferguson, Madeline Jackson, Cheryl Toussaint, and Kathy Hammond had to do well in their heat to qualify for the finals. Cheryl, running the third leg of the relay, waited to receive the baton from Madeline Jackson.

"I turned," Cheryl said, recreating the situation, "and reached for the stick. I was just starting to run with it when a girl from another team fell in front of me. My first reaction was to rear back, so I wouldn't trip over her—but you never stop. I dashed around her, only to have *another* runner step on the heel of my left shoe. Half my shoe was tied on tightly, but the other half was crushed under my heel. 'Oh, my God,' I thought, 'I can't believe it. Here I am in the Olympics, and my shoe is coming off!'

"If I had stopped to pull it up, my teammates would have killed me, and I'd have felt awful because that was our opportunity to win a medal. So I just ran. I'd gone another ten yards or so when the shoe flew up in the air. I just kept running, dazed, wondering if my shoe had hit anyone, if the people in the stands and on TV could see my bare foot, and if they were asking what that girl was doing out there without a shoe.

"There had been two teams ahead of us when I got the stick; but somehow, before I knew it, I had passed their runners. Then I saw where I was and I felt stunned at getting there. All I'd been thinking was that my shoe had come off, that this was the Olympics, and that these things don't happen. But it did."

She may have done it the hard way—but she'd done it. Cheryl

and her teammates had made it to the relay finals. "I was really confident," Cheryl said of the finals. "Nothing more could happen after that shoe thing. So when I received the baton pass, I just ran and ran until I couldn't run any more. We took second behind East Germany.

"Getting up on the victory stand with my teammates, I realized that I was going to come home from my first Olympics with a silver medal. Of course, I wish we had won, but that doesn't mean I wasn't thrilled by being up there. And, anyway, there was Montreal in 1976 to look forward to, and maybe a gold medal."

After the '72 Olympics, Cheryl came home and continued to concentrate on school and track. She graduated from college with a B+ average in 1974 and got a job with the Federal Reserve Bank in its management training program. And, at the same time, she started working toward the 1976 Olympics.

Cheryl collected many trophies and prizes in her running career, but the greatest reward track gave to the skinny girl from Bedford-Stuyvesant was a chance at a whole new life. For Cheryl, being one of Freddy's Atoms spelled the difference between being nobody and being somebody very special.

Fred Thompson might have known it all along, but Cheryl didn't realize just how special she was until February 5, 1970, when she set the first of her several world records. "It was in Toronto, Canada," she recalled, "at the Maple Leaf Invitational Indoor Games. I had never run the 600-yard event before in my life, but I felt prepared because I had been training well.

"There were so many girls in the event that it was split into two heats, both to count as finals. That meant you could win your heat and still lose the race if the girls in the other section had faster times. I was in the second section and my goal was to beat the time of the winner in the first heat.

"There were three and three-quarter laps to run in all, and, with about two laps left, I heard Freddy yelling, 'Go! Go! What are you waiting for?' And I went!

"I won my heat, then walked around the track to where Freddy and my teammates were waiting. It was funny, everybody was jumping up and down and smiling and reaching out to me. I looked at them and asked, 'Did I win?' What I meant was, did I beat the fastest time of the first heat? They just kept smiling. Then Freddy said, 'Look up at the clock.' So I looked and the clock read 1:22.2. I said, 'That's nice, I won.' Freddy just kept looking at me and said very calmly, 'I think it's a new world record.'

"I thought he was kidding, until they announced it over the loudspeaker. Then the tears came. I was so excited, and I couldn't believe it. I just could never imagine that *I* had really broken a world record—me, who'd never run a 600 before, who had never, never thought of myself as a world-record-holder. It was too much for me to understand. Freddy was overjoyed, and I was, too. I can't even express all the feelings I had. They told me to jog a victory lap, and I went around the track crying, with my mind in a total fog. At that moment, I felt as if I'd never be tired, as if I could run forever.

"That night, after I'd calmed down a little, I thought about it. Lots of people break world records, but *me*—wow! I thought about how lucky I was to be an Atom, and of all the things it had given me, and it was so wonderful."

Jenny Bartz/Lynn Genesko
Nina MacInnis/Sharon Berg
SWIMMING

For some reason, America's great female swimmers always seemed to reach the peak of their competitive careers in their mid-teens and to retire a few years later. Yet top women competitors from other parts of the world swam on, often setting records well into their twenties.

American swimming observers had lots of theories to explain the fast-fading American women. Some said that as girls became women, developing breasts and wide hips, they could no longer cut through the water with the same speed. Others claimed that American teenagers were more interested in boys than in sports and didn't want to seem unfeminine by being competitive. And still others suggested that women just weren't emotionally suited for the single-minded discipline required for world-class swimming competition.

None of these explanations seemed to be sufficient, however. After all, women from other parts of the world found that changes in their bodily proportions didn't keep them from winning; many of them had married and even had children without giving up competitive swimming; and they seemed to cope well emotionally with the demands of the sport. Why could these women continue to win when Americans gave up so young?

The answer is that many American girls quit swimming early simply because they lacked the opportunity. As long as they were in high school and swimming for top AAU clubs around the country, they could devote the necessary time and effort to their sport. But those who went on to college found no women's swimming team and no financial or emotional support. Those who got jobs were unable to find enough time for the long practice sessions they needed to keep up with the competition. In fact, it was difficult—if not impossible—to swim competitively after high school. The system was set to discard girls at 17 or 18.

Prodded by the women's liberation movement, the swimming establishment began to question the absurdly unfair situation. The answer was clear: provide athletic scholarships for women and encourage the swimmers to keep on competing. Of course, even in the past, some schools *had* offered athletic scholarships to women. But those were of little value because the rules of organized swimming placed strict limitations on the swimmers' eligibility to compete as amateurs.

Finally, in 1973, college scholarship eligibility rules were changed, and four young women were invited to join the University of Miami swimming team. They became the first American females ever to receive nationally recognized swimming scholarships. Bill Diaz, the Miami swimming coach, had made a serious effort to find just the right people for his allotted scholarships. "I wanted one for each stroke," he explained. "So I got on the phone, calling coaches of AAU teams, asking which top-flight girls were graduating from high school. I was looking for the perfect combination—mature girls who were good college material and strong swimmers."

By the summer of 1973 coach Diaz had his team assembled: individual medleyist Jenny Bartz; breaststroker Lynn Genesko; butterflyer Nina MacInnis; and freestyler Sharon Berg.

Four girls with different backgrounds and different personalities, coming together in Miami with the same ambitions—to swim and to win. What were these four athletic pioneers like?

If there was a super-superstar among the Miami swimmers, it had to be Jennifer Bartz. An excellent all-around swimmer, she was world-ranked in the individual medley (I.M.), an event in which the swimmer must swim a different stroke on each lap—butterfly, backstroke, breaststroke, and freestyle.

Jenny was born on July 23, 1955, in Delaware, Maryland, where she spent her early years. She began swimming at the age of seven. Her first specialty was the breaststroke. "It was rinky-dink stuff," she said, "until I was ten, when my father entered me in a state 'Y' meet. I was hesitant about entering, because I had never been in any real competition, and it was scary-new. Surprisingly, I took third place in the 50-yard breaststroke. My time was 38.2 seconds or something ridiculous like that, but it made me feel tremendous. I couldn't believe it, that I was third in my state in anything."

A sturdy little girl, Jenny was enthusiastic about anything connected with the outdoors and sports. When she was 13, the Bartzes moved to Sunnyvale, California, making it possible for Jenny to join the famous Santa Clara swim team. By then she was already an emerging star and, with some coaching from

Santa Clara's George Haines, qualified for her first Nationals. "It was the summer of 1968," Jenny remembered years later, "and the meet was held in Lincoln, Nebraska. It was cold and rainy and miserable and frightening. I didn't know anyone or anything. I just stared at Debbie Meyer and the other big stars. I was only 13, so inexperienced, and it showed. I finished 50th in a field of 50 in one of my breaststroke events and not much better in the other. I never felt so awful, ever. I cried most of the time. Nothing has ever been as scary as that, not even the Olympic Trials or the Olympics themselves."

To increase her strength, Jenny followed coach Haines' orders: work on other strokes besides the breaststroke. She practiced diligently and became so fast in every event that she began swimming the I.M., and winning. The seemingly endless practice sessions were a grind, and there was almost no time in her day that wasn't scheduled, but Jenny never complained.

"When I was in high school," she said, "I was up at 5:30. I'd have breakfast, and my mom would get me to the 6:30 practice. I'd finish swimming about 8:00 and go directly to classes. At 1:30 I'd go home, get Mom to drive me to the pool, and have another workout from 2:00 to 4:00. After that, there was homework and dinner and sleep. I went to bed early because I had to be up so early the next day. That was the way it was, and that was the way I wanted it to be."

All that effort seemed to be paying off—until the summer of 1971. To build strength Jenny had been working out three times a day, swimming nearly 50 miles a week. Things had been going well, but suddenly she began losing every race, and losing badly. Tired and discouraged, she considered quitting.

Coach Haines, familiar with swimmers' letdowns, asked Jenny to compete in the Nationals before making any final decisions. He also suggested that she ease up on her training schedule and relax a bit.

Fortunately, Jenny agreed to try it his way—and at the 1971 Summer Nationals in Houston, Texas, she reached the finals in the 400-meter I.M. Still smarting from her string of recent losses, she was not very optimistic about her chances in the finals. So she decided she'd just do her best and then retire. And that was how she felt when the race began.

"Suddenly," Jenny recalled, "I was in front after the butterfly 100. But I dropped back and after the backstroke 100 I was about even with the rest of the girls. In the breaststroke, I pulled about a body length ahead and went into the freestyle trying to keep my lead. Then, coming in on the last lap of the free, I began telling myself, 'God, you're going to win; you're actually going to win!' When I touched the wall, I couldn't even understand what had happened. And my mother was crying so much, she didn't even see my race. She was so happy and proud, and I felt better than I had in my whole life."

Just as suddenly as she had begun her losing streak, Jenny started to put together a string of victories. Winning a Nationals event and gaining number one ranking in the United States was only part of the glory. Jenny also won a spot on the U.S. team that was traveling to Germany and Russia for international competition. It was a valuable competitive experience for the Olympic hopeful—and an exciting first trip abroad.

The Olympic year, 1972, was spent in an all-out effort to make the U.S. team. Jenny, then a high-school junior, lived every day with that one thought, knowing that every other rival in America was doing the same thing. The pressure at the Olympic Trials was almost suffocating, with hundreds of youngsters battling for one of the three spots in each event. Jenny was one of the lucky ones, qualifying for the I.M. But although she did make the finals at Munich, Jenny failed to win a medal.

"What happened to me," she explained, "is what hits a lot of other American swimmers. The competition for our team was so great, and we had trained so hard for that. Tapering down from long-distance to sprints in preparation just for that one big meet created our problem at Munich. Then it was like a letdown because there wasn't time to build and taper for the Olympics. The kids who'd been in earlier Games knew the psychological downer that comes after the Trials and could prepare psychologically. I had been really up for the Trials, and I just couldn't get myself to that peak again.

"I'm not finished, though. I'll be swimming in '76, and I'll know what to do then."

Indeed, Jenny wasn't finished. She continued as a ranked 400 Individual Medleyist in the United States, helped set a number of American relay records, and, while swimming on her much-deserved athletic scholarship at Miami, kept right on as one of her country's greatest swimmers.

Lynn Genesko, born in Woodbridge, New Jersey, on August 19, 1955, was a spirited, intellectually curious little girl. She took an active part in everything—baseball, running races, ballet, piano lessons, football, school—and was enthusiastic about whatever she was doing. Although she was extremely nearsighted and had to wear glasses all the time, Lynn never let it bother her—or prevent her from trying something new.

When she was eight years old, she was given a few swimming lessons at a local "Y," and joined the games and races at a summer swim club. "I never really thought about it much," Lynn said. "Swimming was just something among a lot of things to do. Then, when I was about eleven, I was watching a swim meet on TV, and I turned to my dad and said, 'That's what I want when I grow up.' I don't know whether I was serious or not, but my father took me to Rutgers University, where the Central Jersey team trained. Frank Elm, the coach, said, 'Get in the water and let's see.' So I did, and he said, 'Mmmm, maybe.' And that was it! I loved it."

Unlike many swimmers who start with one favorite stroke, then change as they grow, Lynn was always a breaststroker. For a couple of months, she swam only twice a week, while her coach waited to see if she was really serious. Then Lynn went on a four-days-a-week, 1½-hours-a-day practice schedule. After a few months of that training, she entered her first meet and, to her astonishment, won a gold medal.

"It was absolutely freaky," she said, "to get a win so fast. It was the 100-yard breaststroke, long for a kid in a first race, but it felt like nothing. I was so psyched up after that, I thought I was the greatest swimmer in the world. All my fantasies went to work."

Lynn wanted to be a great swimmer, but her "million other interests" kept getting in the way. She was the girl who wanted to do it all—write for the school newspaper, run track, get perfect grades, join every club, read every book in the library, play a dozen different sports. To stay focused on swimming, her favorite activity, Lynn depended on her family.

"They've had so much to do with it," she said, "that I could never claim that it's been all me. It's also a part of them. For all those years, I used to wonder if my little sister hated me, because it was me that got all the attention. The whole family wrapped its life around my swimming."

Lynn was extremely close to her father, and she tried to do things that would please him. Mr. Genesko gave Lynn the kind of attention many fathers reserve for their sons, expecting her to succeed in sports, cheering her up when she was in a slump, setting up extra work schedules.

The Central Jersey team had only one practice session a day, so Lynn's father took her to a "Y" early each morning for an extra hour in the water. "I could dog it during team practice," Lynn said, "because I was counting my own laps. But with my dad doing the timing and counting in those morning sessions, I didn't get away with anything. I'd go all-out, while he'd time me in the 100 or 200 breaststroke. Then when I was finished, he'd say, 'Do it again, faster.' I'd feel as if my lungs were about to burst, but I'd do it again, and I *would* go faster. I'd be furious at him, but he was always right. And of course, I knew I needed his help. I'd beg him to take me—and complain when he did."

With more hard work and experience, Lynn's swimming improved. At the age of 14 she won the Eastern Championships in the 100-meter breaststroke. "It was unforgettable," Lynn said with a grin. "I got out of the pool in an absolute daze. I didn't believe I had won. My teammates were crowding around, and there were lots of other people, too, and they were all

68

congratulating me. I was so confused that I thought I was in the locker room, and I started taking off my bathing suit. It was down to my waist before I realized where I was. Unforgettable!"

Though Lynn's smooth, fast swimming took her to the Nationals year after year, the sport gave her more than just medals. She swam for her father's pleasure, and for her own, enjoying the wonderful physical feeling of swimming. "I was in track, too," Lynn said, "until it hurt my legs for swimming. But the two sports are a lot alike. It's all your own—you against the clock. There's the feeling of pushing your body to the limit, making it work for you. You swim hard and begin to hurt, and then you swim with the pain and over the pain. Sometimes I think swimmers are masochists, who don't feel good unless they feel awful. I feel best when I've worked so hard that I ache and can hardly stand."

Lynn was also swimming toward a reward: the 1972 Olympics. But first she had to qualify for the American Trials. In a moment of heartbreak, she missed the cut-off time by a hundredth of a second—and quit swimming. In her senior year at Woodbridge High School, she let her cropped "swimmer's hair" grow long. It was her way of saying she was really through.

By the end of that year, however, Lynn realized how much she had missed the pool—the fun, the pain, the competition. She had already decided to try again when she was offered the scholarship to Miami, which she accepted with wholehearted enthusiasm. "My attitude had been so wrong," Lynn admitted. "I always felt I was swimming for others, but I finally saw that I had to swim for me, that I had to do well for me. Now I have something to prove to myself."

Sharon Berg, Jenny Bartz,
Nina MacInnis and ***Lynn Genesko*** (top to bottom)
pose at the University of Miami swimming pool.

In a 1973 relay race, Lynn Genesko prepares her take off as Jenny Bartz reaches for the wall as she finishes her lap.

At Miami, with only herself and her coach to push her, Lynn started proving herself to be a champion.

The daughter of a Delaware River pilot, Nina MacInnis was a true water baby. Born on June 6, 1954, she began swimming without ever taking lessons at an early, unremembered age. "My family belonged to a summer club that had swimming races for all the kids," she said. "It was very informal, and nobody worried about technique. It was just fun. One day, the summer I was six, my club's team needed one more girl for the eight-years-and-under relay, so I volunteered. Each one had to swim freestyle one length [25 yards] of the pool. When my turn came, I belly-flopped into the water. I couldn't swim very well, but we won. I felt so great, and that was it—then and there."

For the next two years Nina swam only during the summers. Then she joined an all-year age-group AAU team in Philadelphia. But even then, swimming was more of a hobby than the way of life it would soon become. Compared to her schedule in later years, those early times seemed a lark—only two hours a day, four days a week.

"The first time I was serious about swimming was when I was ten," Nina recalled. "My goal was to beat a particular girl who swam for another team and who was number one in the ten-and-under age group. Finally, at one meet, I was entered in the same 50-yard butterfly event as she. I asked my dad whether, if I beat her, he'd buy me real stockings, which I wanted very much. He said yes because he didn't believe I could do it. Well, I beat her. I did a faster time than I had ever done—and I got my stockings."

Swimming was a real family affair for the MacInnises. Nina and her younger sister and brother all swam. Every weekday Nina's mother drove the kids to the pool (a 45-minute ride each way), waited around while they practiced, and then brought them home. Weekends were reserved for meets.

Little time was left for other sports or extracurricular activities; they simply didn't mix with a swimmer's schedule. "I had another goal once," Nina said. "I wanted to be a gymnast, too. I loved to tumble and such, but then I hurt my back at gymnastics just before a big swim meet and I had to give it up."

Nina was a very gawky 13-year-old when she first qualified for the Nationals. In order to qualify, she had to lower her time in the 200 butterfly (her best event) by four seconds. She practiced constantly, swimming on and on long after her body screamed "Enough!"—seeking the pain that told her it was a good workout. Then, at the special time-trial held for qualification, Nina churned through the water as if her whole existence depended on that one race. She made up those four precious seconds, and then some.

"When I got to that first Winter Nationals in Pittsburgh in 1968," Nina remembered, "I spent the two days before my event walking around, wide-eyed. I was so in awe of the big-name swimmers. I was really in a daze, and I wasn't even nervous on the block. But halfway through the event, I realized where I was, in the *Nationals*, and I just choked. I finished last."

That was the beginning of a frustrating pattern. Twice a year, whenever there were Nationals, Nina would qualify and then do poorly. In the summer of 1970, however, after switching teams and coaches, she began to improve. The Olympics were just two

73

years away, so she had no time to be relaxed or casual about swimming. Nina practiced twice a day, restricted her social life to team activities, and finally broke her Nationals jinx. In the 200 that summer, Nina was fifth in a race that saw the first four finishers break the World record.

Knowing how much she yearned to make the Olympic team, Nina's parents arranged for her to spend a year boarding with a family in Santa Clara, California, the swimming capital of the United States. It was a huge expense, but it seemed the most likely way to turn her dream into a reality. Nina made the most of that year, doing her water work under the direction of coach George Haines and practicing with some of the best swimmers in the country.

"Those practices," Nina recalled, "were so tough. I wasn't one of a few top-ranked swimmers any more, like on the team back East. I had to keep up with a whole batch of world-class kids. Nobody goofed off or cheated on laps by telling the coach that he or she had done 50 when it was really 45, or stuff like that. We did $3\frac{1}{2}$ hours in the pool on school days, and $4\frac{1}{2}$ when there was no school."

Occasionally, the Santa Clara swimmers would find the intense workouts a little *too* serious. Then in the early morning, when the cold dawn fog obscured the warm pool, Nina and her teammates would swim to the far side and hide where the coach couldn't see them. As he'd walk around looking for them, the girls would dive under and away. But mostly it was serious work—sprints, kick laps holding a foam board, pull laps with legs strapped together—thousands of yards each day. And always faster, always harder.

Despite all her hard work, Nina just missed qualifying at the Olympic Trials. Shocked and disappointed, she decided to give up swimming. Feeling lost, and wondering if she had wasted her youth, she did some heavy thinking about the future. For months she was in limbo. She had already graduated from high school, and her parents were begging her to make a decision—to swim or to come home.

Nina finally concluded that it made no sense to give up something she loved just because of one big setback. She decided to try again. "I think I was never really ready for success before I came back," she said. "I used to get to finals and want to run away. My body had been able to do it, but my mind wasn't ready, and so I always psyched myself out of winning. When I came back, for the first time I was swimming because I wanted it more than anything else."

Returning to practice in early 1973, Nina began to show the championship style and speed she had never before attained. Her smooth power and cool competitiveness brought her wins at the 1973 Nationals and Santa Clara Invitational meets, a place on the U.S. team for the World Championships in Yugoslavia—and, of course, her scholarship.

Blonde and freckle-faced Sharon Berg looked like a poster proclaiming, "Come to Sunny California." Sharon was indeed a native of the Golden State. Born June 23, 1955, in Hermosa Beach, she spent her early years just one block away from a pool and the Pacific Ocean. Swimming was almost as natural as walking. "I began taking real swimming lessons when I was about four," Sharon said. "I guess I had a bathing suit, but I learned in underwear. The teacher would throw plastic rings into the pool, and I'd scoot to the bottom to pick them up. I loved diving for those 'donuts,' and the whole thing was delightful. I felt so good in the water. I wasn't ever afraid, it was just so comfortable."

When Sharon was seven she began her competitive career, joining her older sister on a local team. "I always felt confident about swimming," she said, "and that made it easy. My aim was just to stay in the pool, practicing as long as my sister, and to keep up with her and the other bigger kids. And it was fun winning blue ribbons at the meets we had on weekends. There was nothing serious about swimming, though. It was just one of the things we liked."

The Bergs encouraged their daughters to be energetic and physically active. They were delighted when their quiet, introspective younger child did so well in the pool. Until she started swimming, Sharon spent a lot of time alone, reading or studying. Swimming brought her out of herself and made her part of a group.

When Mr. Berg's employer transferred him to Northern California in 1967, the family relocated in Sunnyvale. The move was good for Sharon because it placed her near the home base of the powerful Santa Clara AAU swimming team. She joined the team at twelve and immediately began to compete in America's toughest league. After two years of dedicated work, she qualified for the 1970 Nationals along with teammate and friend Jenny Bartz.

"That was thrilling," she recalled. "Everybody on the team congratulated me, and it was so nice. The Nationals were being held in Ohio, and I got to fly the whole way East. I had qualified in four events—100 and 200 butterfly, 200 freestyle, and 200 I.M.—and I swam them all. I did *my* best times in all of them. I was also in a relay that placed in the top eight, so I got to stand on the award stand.

"I remember getting to the block for my first event, the 100 butterfly. My knees were shaking and my heart was pounding. My mother was in the stands, and she could even see my legs trembling. I didn't really think about the older, better swimmers —just that it was the Nationals, and I was scared!"

Sharon placed among the top 25 in all her individual events and, as the "most improved" swimmer in the group, was given the huge team trophy Santa Clara won in the meet.

A shy, serious teenager, Sharon never objected to the rigid scheduling that shaped her days. She managed to maintain an A average in high school, despite the two exhausting daily sessions in the pool. With a deep religious faith and a desire to always do the right thing, Sharon might cry a bit from the pain of practice, but she'd never let up.

Monday through Saturday were for swimming; Sunday was for church. Sharon willingly gave up a normal teenager's life and all other extracurricular activities. The workouts were draining, with thousands of yards to do, ever faster, but the water was a welcome place. "I don't know why," Sharon said, "but I've always felt comfortable, really at home, in the water. Sometimes, while I'm doing laps, my mind is a million miles off, and a song will go through my head over and over. Often I think about homework, or problems, things that have been bothering me outside of swimming, that have me confused or upset. I'm not always aware that I'm thinking about these things, but then I realize that I've got them worked out in the water. When that happens, I feel great, and I swim even faster."

Twice a year, Sharon competed in the Nationals, getting faster each time. Then in 1972 she made it to the finals, taking seventh place in the 200-meter freestyle. At that same meet she was on a relay team that set a new American record. "We were shouting and crying, and we all jumped in the water," she said. "It was the most exciting moment of my life. It hurts, really hurts, when you go all-out and lose; but when you win, the pain just disappears."

Even though she didn't qualify for the '72 Olympics, Sharon wasn't too disappointed. She had achieved a high national ranking and was young enough to hope for a trip to Montreal in 1976. Then in 1973, the 18-year-old high school senior was offered an athletic scholarship, and she knew the thrill of being a pioneer among female athletes.

Never having lived away from home before, Sharon traveled to the University of Miami feeling like an explorer entering an untouched wilderness. "While I was at home," she said, "my parents always watched everything I did, and I depended on them to help me regulate my life. It wasn't that they pushed; they've always told me, 'Whenever you want to quit, it's fine with us.' But they were there, and, in a way, I was swimming for them. I used to believe that I was imposing on my parents if they came and I didn't do well in a meet. Now it's just me, and that's a good feeling."

Jenny, Lynn, Nina, and Sharon—these were the four young women who came to Florida and revolutionized American swimming. They were leading the way for every girl who dreams about being a great athlete, winning a scholarship, and becoming that rare human being—a champion.

They joined Miami's formerly all-male team and hit the water with burning ambition. Practices twice a day were old stuff. There wasn't a schedule made that could intimidate these veterans. They relished every moment—the freedom of being on their own, the camaraderie of the team, the chance for an education—and most of all, the opportunity for four years of expert training and coaching.

Coach Diaz knew from the start that he had awarded the scholarships wisely. AAU rules restricted the swimmers to racing against their own sex in meets, but for everything else, the team—boys and girls—was a unit.

"It's good for all of them socially," Diaz explained. "It builds team spirit, and it helps everyone's swimming. In general, I find that girls are more mature than boys of the same age. The girls are extremely serious about their swimming and schoolwork. They are very dedicated and not likely to break training. Because of these characteristics, they're good scholarship material—and an excellent influence on the boys."

To get the most out of all his swimmers, coach Diaz had the girls swim in the same lanes as the boys. Because boys usually do faster times, the girls had to swim harder to keep up than if they had been isolated in separate lanes. Keeping up became a matter of pride, as well as a physical necessity. Slow up, and someone would swim into you or over you. Self-preservation demanded speed from the girls.

And how did the boys on the Miami squad feel? David

Wilkie, the Scottish breaststroker who won a silver medal for Great Britain at the 1972 Olympics, said, "It's good having them at workouts, because they *do* train hard. Sometimes they show us up, and if they beat us, we feel bad. So having them here makes us work harder."

Todd Ford, who had graduated from an all-boys high school, called the coed team "fabulous." Chris McKee, accustomed to swimming with girls on an AAU team, thought it was natural and normal. "Of course, I don't want to be passed by a girl," Chris said, "but I don't want to be passed by *any*one."

As coach Diaz said, "Putting them all together helps everyone. It also makes a coach's life a lot easier. They're doing all the work."

It began with four girls at one school. But in the years that followed, women were awarded more and more athletic scholarships from more and more colleges. The future had begun with Nina, Jenny, Lynn, and Sharon—pioneers who cut a path through the water that would be swum by thousands of girls in the years ahead.

Paula Sperber
BOWLING

It was the last frame of the last game of the 1971 women bowlers' U.S. Open, and Paula Sperber was 20 points behind her opponent. With $4,000 top-prize money in the balance, she stepped to the line. Settling the ball in her left hand, she looked at the triangle of ten pins at the other end of the lane, took a deep breath, and began her approach. The black ball flew from her hand, streaked down the lane, and cracked into the pins, knocking them all down. Strike! She was still in the contest, but she'd have to make the most of her two bonus balls if she hoped to win. Paula waited impatiently for the ball to come back, then quickly lifted it from the return rack, stepped to the line, and sent it spinning toward the pins. Another strike! Again she waited; again she took the ball, got set, and let it go. Nine pins on her final throw (29 points on the final frame) and a total of 215 for the game.

Now Paula sat down to watch her opponent, June Llewellyn, try to beat her. All Ms. Llewellyn needed was nine pins to tie—and ten to win. Her first ball knocked down eight pins and left two standing far apart—a split that was extremely difficult to make. Going for broke, Ms. Llewellyn tried to convert the split—and missed both pins. She finished with a total of 214, one pin behind Paula.

Paula Sperber was the champion. It was a goal she had never even considered when she began bowling. In fact, if it hadn't been for her mother, Paula might never have become involved in the sport at all. In 1962 Josephine Sperber was being treated for bursitis. "Try bowling," the doctor advised. "It's good exercise for your condition." So that very evening, Josephine and her husband, Joseph, agreed to go bowling. Not wanting to leave their youngest daughter home alone, they took eleven-year-old Paula along.

Born on March 1, 1951, in Miami, Florida, Paula was a natural athlete who did well at all games. "I was always outside," she said, "playing with the neighborhood kids. I never liked dolls or that stuff. Also, it wasn't completely a matter of choice; it was more that where we lived, all the other kids were boys. My sisters [Marion and Marcia, six and eight years older than Paula] were too old to be my playmates, and there were no other girls around. So if the boys played football, I played football, too—or softball or volleyball. Whatever they did, I wanted to do. In a way, I was one of the guys."

Paula had bowled before she went with her parents that night. Marcia and Marion had occasionally taken their kid sister along when they went bowling with their friends. They would allow her to roll one frame (two balls), just to keep her quiet. But being allowed to bowl game after game with her parents was a new and wonderful experience.

The athlete in Paula responded to the sport's challenge. After that first outing, she repeatedly begged her parents to let her come with them to bowl or even just to watch. As she later recalled, "I had some huge fights with my father. They'd go out on week nights, bowling in a league with their friends, and it would last until 11 o'clock or so. Of course, I had school the next day, and they wanted me to be in bed earlier. But I'd plead and beg and wheedle, and Dad usually gave in."

Later that year Paula joined a league herself, and began weekend age-group competition. As an under-twelve "bantam" bowler, she felt no real pressure to win, just the gratification of playing a game with other youngsters. There was something else, though, that the sport gave to thin, pre-adolescent Paula. Shortly before Paula discovered bowling, the neighborhood boys began joining school teams and became less willing to include her in their games. None of the girls in her class lived nearby, and her teenage sisters had their own groups and interests. So, when bowling captivated their youngest child, the Sperbers recognized its value and encouraged her to participate. The bowling center was jammed with boys *and* girls every weekend, and it seemed like a good place for Paula to make some new friends.

"My average was really awful when I first started," Paula said, "but it didn't matter. It was about 107, or was it 97? Anyway, what really counted was the fun of doing it. I wanted to do well, like I've always wanted to do well in any sport, but not to the point of worrying if I didn't. Each year I'd improve, with the experience of doing it over and over, but I certainly wasn't a great champion as a bantam or junior bowler."

For the first two years, Paula used one of the "house" balls stocked by the bowling center. Recapturing the feelings of those years, Paula said, "I wanted my own ball so badly, but my parents kept saying that I wasn't ready. They were right, because a kid's fingers grow so fast that it's just too complicated and expensive to keep redrilling the ball and plugging it. Still, I wanted it, and that was all I could think of. There was one special ball that I thought of as mine, and I'd rush to get to the lanes early, way before my league, so nobody would get it first. It was a kind of lucky ball for me. I felt I bowled better with this one than any other. Actually, with my scores, it couldn't have been so lucky. But that wasn't the way I saw it then."

When Paula was about 13 years old and had been bowling for two years, she discovered a way to get a bowling ball of her own. A magazine company was offering a ball to any youngster who could sell four $10 subscriptions to *The Saturday Evening Post*. The problem was that none of the subscriptions could be sold to a relative, and Paula doubted that she could convince four strangers to buy them. Nevertheless, she decided the ball was worth the effort. Canvassing her neighborhood from house to house, Paula finally reached her quota.

"When that ball arrived," she said, giggling at the memory, "I thought it was the most beautiful thing I'd ever seen. It weighed eleven pounds and was just perfect. I felt so important the next weekend, going bowling with my own ball. It had to be luckier than *any* house ball."

Even with her lucky ball, Paula never dreamed of becoming a champion. "Like all kids," she said, "I'd bowl erratically. When I was concentrating, my score would go up. Then my mind would begin to wander, and it would show in my control and accuracy. Maybe, though, it should be that way with kids in sports.

There's so much pressure on children today to do everything expertly. It's better if a sport is played for kicks when you're young. There's always time to be serious about it later, when it really counts. If I had worked hard and concentrated hard when I was young, I might have been better now. But I might also have given it up, because it would have been work instead of play, at an age when I wanted to enjoy myself."

Fortunately, Paula managed to enjoy herself *and* improve her game. Not long after she got her own ball, she achieved her first triumph, being named Young Bowler of the Week in a citywide survey. Every week, a young bowler with the highest score in Miami would be awarded that title, along with the chance to compete at year's end against the other 51 weekly winners. The final tournament proved to be a surprisingly scary experience for Paula.

"I didn't worry about it before," she said, "but when I got there I was trembly. I hadn't practiced for the tournament, though I don't think that would have changed anything. I did really poorly that time, and I felt a little sorry, but not too much. I enjoyed the game."

Despite the fact that Paula rolled one 200 game that same year, her average was only about 130. But since she never intended to make the sport more than a relaxing hobby, she didn't worry much about her score. Then in 1966, when she was 15 years old and rolled a 290—just ten pins short of perfection—Paula began to take bowling more seriously.

That year Paula won her first tournament. Sponsored by a local newspaper, it was, like the earlier one, a citywide contest for young bowlers. She was thrilled with her success and the trophy she won. That was something she could take to school for all to see. "It was like Show and Tell," she said, laughing, "with me doing all the showing and telling. I really felt great."

After Paula graduated from Citrus Grove Junior High School, the family began looking for a larger home. Carl Park High School had an excellent bowling team, and it was partly to give Paula the opportunity to join it that the Sperbers moved there. Paula looked forward to the move, but it turned out to be more upsetting than she had expected. She especially missed her school friends and the familiar neighborhood in which she had lived her whole life. At Carl Park, Paula knew no one and felt awkward and out-of-place.

The move was not without some advantages, however. Miami is one of the few areas in the United States where bowling is a varsity sport, and Paula's transfer to the district with the finest team was an important step toward her future career. And through her membership on the school team, Paula began making friends.

"I had met some of the girls before, bowling in the junior traveling league," she explained. "In fact, it was through them that we moved. These girls told my parents that if I went to Carl Park and bowled on the team, we'd probably be able to win the city championship. Mom and Dad had talked about moving, and this clinched it."

At her new school, Paula's skill at stringing strikes and her easygoing personality finally brought her acceptance. Yet she never felt as comfortable there as she had in her old neighborhood. "I guess I had a hand in the decision," she admitted, "but if I had known how hard it would be, I would never have moved. And I'd never do it with a kid of mine. The sport, any sport, can be important, but it's not as important as feeling happy and that you belong when you're an adolescent.

"I had the roughest three years of my life then. The school was nice, and the teachers were great. I was an honor roll student, so that was no problem. It was the atmosphere that bothered me. The school was full of clubs—the main reason for which was *ex*cluding people—and I wanted no part of that. So I went to classes, and worked with the bowling team every day—and that was it."

When she wasn't at school, Paula spent no time with her schoolmates. Her sisters and mother were her girlfriends, and her boyfriends were "older men" whom she met through her sisters. For two years she went steady with a boy who also was a bowler, and they spent many of their dates at a local bowling alley.

Paula had an open, warm relationship with her family, and she felt secure and trusted at home. Years afterward, she said that she always remained grateful to her parents for treating her as a grownup with a mind of her own, even when she disagreed with them. "I was a pretty straight kid, and I never did anything bad—that they knew about," she said with a grin. "There are some things that parents don't have to know about. Anyway, I never did anything that I thought was wrong, and that was what counted."

Bowling three times a week on her own time, and every day with the school team, Paula improved steadily. Each year her average went up by about ten pins. She never again reached that high of 290, but, more significantly, her bowling was no longer an erratic hit-and-miss routine. Experience was bringing the

Paula Sperber displays her championship form
(left) and poses for a publicity photo (below).

consistency that marks the true champion in any sport.

When Paula was 18, her average reached a plateau of 180, and she couldn't seem to raise it no matter what she tried. She had never been coached, preferring to pick up bowling technique by watching other, more proficient players or by casually discussing her game with local pros.

In 1970 Paula turned pro. She was attending Miami-Dade Junior College at the time, uncertain of what her future would be and hesitant about pinning her hopes on bowling. Going to school and competing on the professional tour part-time were difficult, but Paula had won $210 as a "guest" on a tour in 1969 and was eager to see if she could win more. Bowling as a pro while still attending school, she won only two local tournaments in 1970. It wasn't a very exciting showing for Paula, who remained stuck at the 180 level. However, this lack of success made her realize that she did need coaching, and led to a big breakthrough.

In January 1971 Paula went to Mike Praznovsky, a local bowling pro—left-handed, as she was—and asked him for help. Mike watched her bowl, analyzing her approach, swing, and delivery. Then he set up a training plan. He was certain that Paula had the talent to be a winner—*if* she would make some drastic changes in her style.

"The shot she had was destroying her game," Mike explained. "She was too far toward the middle. But with her amazing strength she could still shatter the pins. And with her average—well, everyone thought she was on the right track. It disturbed me, but I didn't say anything for a long time."

To compensate for the unique hook southpaw Paula had,

Praznovsky finally instructed her to start from a position on the left side of the lane. Paula was skeptical about the wisdom of the move, convinced that every shot she rolled would end in one of the gutters alongside the lane. But her lack of progress had so frustrated her that she was ready for anything, even this. Again and again, Paula would step to the middle of the lane, move left five boards, make her approach, and throw. Again and again, the ball would roll into the gutter. Still Mike assured her that it would work eventually, so Paula kept on with the "silly" new way. Then, amazingly, it all began to fall into place, and the ball started going where she wanted it to go.

Achieving some success encouraged Paula—and then Mike changed things again, moving her *another* five boards to the left. "Which lane do you want me to bowl in?" Paula asked in annoyance. "You've got me so far to the left I'm almost out in the street."

Mike laughed and asked her to trust him. "She thought I was crazy," he said, "but she tried it. And half an hour later she said, 'You know, you're right.' I knew she wouldn't have any trouble. With her strength and coordination she throws the most explosive ball of any girl bowler I've ever seen. I think she could outdo any girl in almost any sport she put her mind to.

"If she wanted to make bowling her life, her obsession, she undoubtedly would be the greatest bowler in the world. But she doesn't. When I first began coaching her, I asked if she was ready for total dedication, and she said she didn't know, that maybe she wanted more out of life than just bowling. At least she was honest."

Paula always hated to practice, to discipline herself to the drudgery of working out alone. "I want to bowl well," she acknowledged, "but I can't stand bowling by myself, without any competition. I'd go to a local bowling center sometimes, determined to keep at it, but I'd get so bored that it was no use. Then people would come over and chat about their game. I enjoyed that—helping someone else or just having a conversation—but it sure was no help for *my* game. That's always been my problem. I'll happily bowl endlessly in any tournament any day, but I just can't practice!"

Nevertheless, after a few months of Praznovsky's coaching, Paula's average jumped to 195. Now she was consistently drilling the ball into the strike "pocket" and sending the pins flying against each other, tumbling like rows of dominoes. And she was picking up spares with more regularity, too.

Then Mike added one more thing: a specially designed glove to support her left wrist and hand. At first, Paula balked at this innovation, too, but experience had proved that Mike knew what he was talking about. So, without too much grumbling, Paula started using the glove. And off she went on the 1971 women's professional bowling tour.

Paula was not very popular with the older women on the tour. Partly, she realized, it was a conflict of generations. The pros who had spent years working at the sport now found themselves overshadowed by a relatively inexperienced kid. And, in Paula's case, it wasn't just her skill that drew attention. A striking 5-foot-6, 125-pound 20-year-old, with enormous blue-grey eyes, a pretty face and long, shiny, blonde hair, Paula was an instant sensation. Dressed in bright, miniskirted outfits made by her mother, she started the tour buzzing. Spectators flocked to watch her, ignoring others, because she was so attractive. But whether the fans came to admire her legs or her bowling, Paula was clearly their favorite. Not surprisingly, some of the older women on the tour resented the newcomer. There was nothing Paula could do about the situation, however, so she just shrugged it off and kept to herself. She knew that she was there to bowl, and to win, and for that she needed only herself.

Paula bowled each tournament with more care than she had ever given to anything in her life. "I really thought about what I was doing—for once," she said. "My approach tends to be too fast, throwing off my shot. So I slowed it by timing my four steps evenly. Too often, bowlers take two slow steps, because they're aware that they should be slower. Then they get all caught up with the delivery, and the last two or three steps speed up and blow the whole thing. I learned to keep an even beat, like in music, and that did it."

In '71 Paula was a leader in every tournament she entered, dazzling audiences, winning purses, and psyching out opponents with her coolness. Then came the U.S. Open, the biggest pro tournament of all. It was held in Kansas City, Kansas, and Paula entered with the uncertain hope of making the finals. Others were more confident about her chances, and many were betting she'd take the title. AMF, a leading manufacturer of bowling equipment, had spotted her as a rising star, and invited her to join its "stable" of bowlers to endorse its products and put on bowling exhibitions. Paula asked the company to wait until after the Open, when she could think about her future more clearly.

"I had been fourth in one tournament and sixth in another, right before Kansas City," Paula remembered, "and I guess maybe I did have some confidence in myself. And when I saw the prize list for the Open, I really wanted to win. I'd made $900 for that other fourth place, while fourth in this one was worth $1,500, and that was my goal. I sure didn't expect to do better. Then the tournament began and things were going very well. I called my parents back home to let them know that I had made it to the final day's matches. After that I couldn't get to a phone until the whole thing was over."

Recalling her dramatic one-point victory over June Llewellyn, Paula said, "It was so exciting. I just sat there watching at the end, and my mind was a total blank. It took me about a week to realize that I had won. In a field of 128 top women bowlers, I had won!"

With the $4,000 first-place purse in the U.S. Open and the "cashing" in other tournaments that year, Paula's 1971 earnings totaled $15,000. But her most precious prize was the title of Woman Bowler of the Year, awarded annually to the outstanding woman on the tour. Paula also was delighted that she had not signed a contract with AMF before the Open. "My price for joining was double their first offer, after I won," she said. "Of course, I might have been a total disaster in the Open, and they still would have signed me, but at so much less and without the $1,000 bonus for the Open. Anyway, it worked out just right."

Paula's life changed greatly after that victory. AMF wanted the attractive young bowler to travel around the world as its representative. To do so, Paula quit school, having completed two years of college. "I'm not sorry I left college," she said, "and I'm not sorry I went for those two years. I had taken lots of English and speech courses, and they really helped me once I was traveling and meeting people and making speeches. And I don't feel that because I'm not in school, I'm not getting an education. Life is learning; going new places and doing new things is learning, too."

Being on the road was fun, but Paula got lonely for her family whenever she was away. She liked having her mother along on trips, and Josephine Sperber did travel with her daughter whenever possible. "I like the women on the tour," Paula explained, "but I'm more comfortable when I'm with someone who knows me well, and who understands my moods. Mom is also a safety factor. Some local 'lover boy' may see me bowl in some city, and phone me at my motel or just hang around. There's never any harm in it, but it can be a nuisance. So when one calls my room and my *mother* answers, the problem just goes away."

Most of the time, however, Paula toured alone. She spent a fortune on long-distance calls to Miami, phoning from as far away as Japan. Each year she divided her time between touring the competition circuit, traveling for AMF, and relaxing at home. When she was in Miami, Paula lived with her parents. "My mother is sort of my private secretary," she said, "because there's an awful lot of correspondence and I'm away so much. She takes care of all that, and she still makes my bowling costumes. There are times when living with my parents is a bit of a pain, like when they're overprotective and tell me what I should do when I haven't even asked. But it's usually rather nice. And I do have fun bowling with them."

Paula and her friend Don Carter, the pro known as "Mr. Bowling," spent much of their leisure time together in Miami.

Both sports nuts, they could be found on the golf course or at the tennis court every free day. Four evenings a week the two pros bowled in local leagues. "Three of my leagues are 'classics,' with top competitors," Paula said, "but another one is my parents' league, and that can be funny. The other team will show up, see Don's name or mine, and turn pale. It's a hospital league, made up of people who work in all the Miami hospitals. My mother is a volunteer at one of the hospitals, and that's how we got into it. The others have averages from about 90 and up, but they're all good-natured about us once they understand that we're not there to kill them. But people do have funny reactions sometimes.

"What I love most about bowling, besides the money I earn," Paula continued, "is that it is open to anyone. I can bowl against the best or the worst, and it's the same pleasure. I can take my sister's kids bowling, and they'll each perform at a different level, but they'll all enjoy it. You don't have to be big and muscular, or a terrific jock, or very rich. It doesn't take all day, the way golf does, and it doesn't require the running of tennis. You can bowl alone, or with any number, and you're always competing against yourself and trying to improve your own score. It's the greatest sport there is."

Playing the "greatest sport" was all Paula wanted to do for a few years, but not forever. She hoped to win the Open again; yet she felt that her real job was carrying the message for America's favorite participant sport. Increasingly, her concern was to make other young women see opportunities in competitive bowling, and to raise the purses in women's tournaments.

A top male bowler can earn $100,000 in a year, while the best female may make one-quarter of that. This unfair money ratio bothered Paula. Why should she bowl as hard, travel as much, and earn so much less than the men?

She set out to upgrade the sport, and the role of women in it. "People do enjoy watching women compete," she argued. "Just look at Billie Jean King's audiences. Maybe they're interested in legs or short skirts to start, but then they get caught up in the excitement of the game.

"It's all tied together. People like to see high purse tournaments, and television stations like to cover them. Bowling sponsors have to understand that the publicity they want comes only with big winnings. Offer a good purse, and have a group of sharp, attractive women bowlers competing for it—it draws the fans. All we need is the chance, and that's what I'm fighting for."

Cathy Rigby
GYMNASTICS

On December 12, 1952, in Long Beach, California, Anita Rigby gave birth to a little girl. The baby, named Cathy, was two months premature and weighed a scant four pounds. Because of her prematurity and two collapsed lungs, the infant was placed in an incubator. There she was watched carefully by her doctors and nurses, although they all held little hope for her survival. Cathy's parents, however, hadn't given up. They already had two healthy children, and they refused to accept the doctors' gloomy prediction. Both mother and father *knew* their little girl would make it.

The parents were right! Cathy survived, soon gaining enough weight and recovering from her lung problems sufficiently to be taken home. But her battle wasn't over—it was just beginning. A fragile infant, susceptible to constant colds and fevers, she was hovered over by her adoring parents.

For the first five years of her life, Cathy was sick more often than she was well. Her weak lungs were repeatedly attacked by infection, causing siege after siege of pneumonia and bronchitis. Each of the many times she was hospitalized the family would be told that this was the end. Still filled with unquenchable faith and confidence, they refused to believe it or let tiny Cathy believe it. "We almost lost her several times," her mother remembered, "but she always came back. Cathy and I are very close and a lot alike. I don't admit defeat in anything, and neither does she."

Then, when Cathy was five years old, something miraculous happened—she got well. Although much smaller than other girls her age and very delicate in appearance, Cathy suddenly developed into a vibrant, healthy youngster. Nevertheless, five years of serious illness always leave a mark, and Cathy was no exception to that rule. In this instance, there were two psychological results: because she had been so coddled by her doting parents, Cathy was a very spoiled and willful child; and, having defeated the repeated threats of death, she seemed to feel that she was indestructible.

As her mother later said, "She was so goldarned active. Always on top of the refrigerator. Even when she fell, she would just climb back up again. There were many times when she cracked her head open, and we were forever rushing her to the emergency room at the hospital. I think she is so fearless because I never believed in giving my children anything to worry about. I never said, 'Don't do that, you'll get hurt.' "

Her mother's attitude, combined with her own experience, had created a little girl with a will of iron. The headstrong youngster seemed determined to show everyone that she was braver and more daring than any other child in the world.

"I'll show you just how strong I am," she seemed to be saying as she taught herself to roller skate, trying every trick possible on eight wheels. But that was easily mastered and soon became too tame for her. Next, the gutsy five-year-old decided to learn to ride a two-wheel bicycle. Tiny Cathy, her feet barely toe-touching the pedals, fell off again and again—and got right back on again and again. Bruises and scrapes and bloody knees and elbows were meaningless. She was intent on riding better and faster than anyone else.

Bike riding became a snap after a while. Yet that, too, once conquered, didn't give Cathy the satisfaction she craved. She was searching for the one activity that would prove to be an endless challenge, something that would demand more and more of her. *That,* and only that, would be the activity she could accept.

Except for her constant activity—jumping off swings in mid-air, climbing anything in sight, and charging headlong at every physical obstacle—Cathy's early life was fairly normal. She was an average student at school, had the usual number of friends among classmates, joined the Brownies, and fought with her sister Paula (nicknamed Mitchie) and brother Steve.

At the age of eight, Cathy began taking ballet lessons. She found the disciplined movements enjoyable but not acrobatic enough. When she heard that a local youth center was offering classes in trampoline, Cathy begged her father to take her there. Paul Rigby recalled that first lesson as the opening of a door to a new universe for his daughter. "On the very first night," he said, "she was doing backflips!"

Cathy had taken the first leap on the path to the perfect sport for her. She loved the tumbling and worked ceaselessly at it. Her tiny, compact body, the cause of so much teasing from her larger classmates and friends, was now a real advantage. Such a small, muscular body was the perfect instrument for tumbling. Cathy made steady progress, swiftly acquiring all the skills the youth center coach could teach her. When she felt that she was ready for advanced instruction, the coach suggested that Mr. Rigby take Cathy to Bud Marquette, a noted gymnastics coach.

Cathy was close to her eleventh birthday when she met Marquette, the man who was to change her life. "When Cathy came to me in 1963," Marquette said years later, "she came in shorts and bare feet. She looked just like a ragamuffin. All she could do was cartwheels. But in about two months she was better than girls who had been training for two years. She never fooled around. She would have excelled no matter what."

With the same intensity that marked their battles against illness, Cathy and her family threw themselves into gymnastics. The Rigbys were then living in Los Alamitos, close to Marquette's gym in Long Beach. Every day, Anita Rigby would drive Cathy to her lessons, wait until they were over, and bring her home. Mitchie, who was then 14, joined the classes, too. Steve, 13, stayed home to take care of seven-year-old Jeff. Baby Jill, the youngest Rigby, was also a daily commuter to Long Beach. While Cathy worked out, Jill would take her afternoon nap on a mat in a corner of the gym. It was no surprise that Jill, too, later became interested in the sport, having been exposed to it almost from the day she was born.

The sheer will that dominated Cathy's gymnastics performances was simply a way of life in the Rigby household. Circumstances made everybody's life difficult. Anita Rigby ran a busy household with five active children even though she was a victim of polio. She couldn't walk without the aid of crutches or get around without a great amount of pain and effort. Even the daily trip to Long Beach was a hardship. Her mother's stoic, uncomplaining acceptance of her condition made a profound impression on Cathy.

To meet the expenses of belonging to Marquette's Southern California Acro Team (SCAT), pay entry fees to gymnastic competitions, and buy extra practice equipment for home use, the Rigbys sacrificed many luxuries. They even sold their piano to pay for a set of uneven bars for the backyard and had a balance beam specially built for Cathy.

Gymnastics was no longer just a game for the athletic youngster. Of course, she enjoyed it and wanted to do well; but there was something else driving her to succeed. She felt she owed too much to her family to stop even if she wanted to, and she meant to repay them by proving she was worth every penny and every minute they had contributed in her behalf.

Cathy had been a member of the SCATs for only a few months when coach Marquette realized that she could be a champion if she was willing to work toward that goal. She was, definitely! Every weekday after school, Cathy spent four hours at practice, building new skills. Then on Saturdays and Sundays, when other kids rested and played, she put in another seven to nine hours each day. The weekend sessions were devoted to perfecting the techniques she had learned all week.

Cathy improved steadily under Marquette's expert direction. He had a tough, no-nonsense approach to work, and he made it clear that he was the boss and that his rules were never to be broken. Marquette offered to show Cathy how she could use her acrobatic daring to win medals, and he was ready to teach her everything he knew. In return, he demanded complete obedience from his pupil. Cathy accepted the terms of the "contract," and was totally under Marquette's authority for the rest of her high-flying career.

As time passed, Cathy began to fill the Rigby living room with trophies. Her specialty was the balance beam, a length of wood less than four inches wide and 15 feet long, fixed in place four feet above the floor. Cathy would jump, or vault, onto the beam, then go through a series of steps, jumps, turns, and runs. Some positions had to be held for a few moments without any movement. The entire performance took about a minute and a half and was scored according to the difficulty of the exercises and the skill of the performance. Because of her compact size and build, low center of gravity, and excellent muscle control, Cathy had a natural advantage in this event.

The real key to Cathy's superb balance beam performances, however, was her utter lack of fear. The same daring that had led her to climb everything in sight when she was a small child was now being put to good use. Fear is a factor that hampers many gymnasts on the beam, but Cathy never even seemed to notice that she had no protection between herself and the floor. Although she was accustomed to falling, her self-confidence and Marquette's assurances kept her from toppling off too often.

"Her fear factor is so minimal," Bud Marquette said of his teenage protégé. "That's what makes her so good. It's unbelievable. She's not afraid of anything. There's no hesitation. Other girls will stand up there and say, 'Oh, I don't know.' They'll chicken out. They'll start crying. It might take three weeks before they'll even try it.

"When Cathy does a trick," Marquette said, "she never stops halfway. She always follows through. I could tell her to jump out of a fifth-floor window, and she would do it. Of course, she would expect me to be there to catch her."

Every human being has fears, though, and Cathy was no exception. Until she was almost twelve years old, she sucked her thumb. When she was finally able to break that habit, she became a compulsive nail-biter. The fear was there, inside, but Cathy never let it hold her back.

"There are a lot of things involved," she said. "Balance beam is difficult. It's easy to fall and unpredictable a lot of the time. But one of the biggest things you have to overcome in gymnastics is fear, or you just don't get very far. It's a psychological thing with me. I can't be afraid because Bud doesn't expect me to be afraid."

In 1967, when Cathy was 14 years old, she competed in her first international meet, a pre-Olympics event, held in Mexico City. While she did well on the balance beam, her overall performance wasn't yet up to world standards. There was still much to do: improve her floor exercises, side-horse vaulting, and uneven bar routines; also, add new movements to the beam work, sharpen her skills to a finer point, and tighten her timing. Bud Marquette repeatedly assured Cathy she could be the greatest, and she had complete faith in him.

At the U.S. Olympic trials in 1968, the steadily improving gymnast took fifth place, winning a place on the American team scheduled to meet the world's top competitors in Mexico City. She was our nation's tiniest Olympian: 4-foot-10½, 89 pounds. A charming pixie with soft brown eyes and blonde pigtails, she resembled a real-life version of Peter Pan.

International gymnastic rules state that competitors must be at least 18 years old to compete, but there were provisions that allowed for a waiver of the rule in exceptional cases. At 15, Cathy was indeed an exceptional case; she was too good to leave behind.

When Cathy first appeared in the Olympic Village, dressed in her red-white-and-blue warm-up suit, everyone thought she was the team mascot. She looked so small and young for a world-class athlete and had such a shy smile, that audiences instantly responded to her.

Being on the Olympic team was a tremendous thrill for Cathy, although she knew that her chances of winning a medal were slim. "I don't expect to take anything this year," she said realistically, "unless I have a really good day. But I hope to watch the Czechs and Russians and learn from them. I'm just excited about getting the opportunity to compete here."

Cathy also was delighted to escape from her home chores, especially those of washing dishes and studying Spanish, the subject that gave her the most trouble in school. With mock sadness, she groaned, "I guess I'll miss about two months of high school. My folks sent me my books, but they couldn't fit in my suitcase, so I sent them home."

Since the popular little teenager wasn't really expected to do well, it came as a huge surprise to everyone when she performed far better than most gymnasts in the competition. Although she was only an alternate in the finals, Cathy placed 16th in the all-around scoring—the highest position ever achieved by an American gymnast. That in itself was a victory.

Home from Mexico City, an exuberant Cathy went back to her schoolwork, home chores, and rigorous workouts. There weren't enough hours in the day for Cathy to do everything she'd have liked, and her life was rigidly scheduled. She attended Los Alamitos High School, dashed to the gym for workouts, did her chores, practiced some more on her home equipment, and slept. Marquette set a 10 P.M. curfew for his gymnasts and made sure they kept it by calling their homes every night.

Cathy gave him no trouble, never breaking curfew or any of the team rules. "I get to travel around a lot and meet people from different countries," she said. "That's a social life, too. I think I'd rather do that right now than go to a dance or something like that."

It wasn't only her total devotion to gymnastics that kept Cathy from dating or from seeking other ways to spend her time. There were also her responsibilities at home, which she took very seriously. In 1969 her father lost his aeronautical engineering job. Mr. Rigby earned what he could by doing odd jobs for the City of Long Beach, bartending, or driving a truck. His wife, still severely handicapped by polio, took a full-time job, but it was hard going. And so, among other responsibilities, Cathy had to rush home from the gym each day to cook dinner for the family.

To earn spending money, which her parents could not afford to give her, Cathy babysat for neighbors and saved every penny. This was supplemented by the three dollars a day amateur athletes are given as pocket money when they travel to tournaments. Cathy hoarded these meager savings to buy Christmas presents for the family.

Yet, despite the lack of money, life wasn't bleak in the Rigby house. There was always fun to be had with brothers and sisters,

Cathy Rigby dances
through her floor routine at the
1972 Olympics in Munich.

After winning every women's event in the 1971 World
Gymnastics Championship, Cathy proudly shows
off her trophy. At right, she performs her two
best events—the uneven parallel bars (top)
and the balance beam (bottom).

visiting cousins, and a menagerie of pets. Roaming through the rooms and underfoot were ducklings, a gopher snake, a dog, a desert tortoise, and Cathy's favorites, Amo the monkey and Beauregard Frump the alligator.

In 1970 all of Cathy's hard work began to pay off. At the World Games, staged in Yugoslavia, she took a silver medal in the balance beam competition. It was the first time an American woman had ever won any medal in international gymnastics, and the accomplishment brought Cathy wide acclaim. Now there was even more incentive to work hard for the 1972 Olympics. And with Cathy's fortunes on the rise, Bud Marquette began to put even stronger pressures on her. She accepted the work because it heightened her chances of winning an Olympic medal, but it took everything the headstrong teenager had to keep from rebelling.

Cathy graduated from high school in 1970 and enrolled in Long Beach State College, but she soon dropped out. The Olympics were coming too close for her to spend time any way but practicing gymnastics. Working seven hours a day now, with only an occasional Sunday off, Cathy began to dream of all the things she would do once the Games were over. "After the Olympics," she said, "I might try skydiving. That would really scare me. They would probably have to push me out of the plane, and I would hope they'd push me. You know Bud would already have told everybody, 'She can do it.' "

Her list of things to do after Munich also included skiing, horseback riding—and getting married. Cathy had secretly started dating Tommy Mason, a professional football player. Marquette insisted publicly that Cathy never dated, and when he learned about Mason he was furious. His control over Cathy was starting to weaken, and he feared that her Olympic gymnastic performance would suffer. As the trip to Munich drew nearer, Cathy was forbidden to see Mason. Marquette was not going to allow anything, including love, to interfere with his plans.

Other conflicts arose. Cathy was beginning to balk at her Barbie Doll image. She was a young women now and very aware of it. Yet she was dieting to keep her weight under 93 pounds, bleaching to hide the darkening of her blonde hair, and wearing the girlish pigtails that were so tight they gave her headaches. She objected, but not strongly. "I would like to let my hair grow," she sighed, "but Bud wouldn't let me."

Gymnastically, Cathy was maturing day by day. In 1971 she won a gold medal at a grand competition in the U.S.S.R.—the first non-Russian ever to do so. In Japan, South Africa, wherever she went, she was a star. Then, on June 5, 1971, Cathy completely dominated the World Cup Gymnastics Champion-ships, held at Miami Beach, Florida. Scoring 38.35 out of a possible 40 points, Cathy captured all the women's events.

Marquette's "little girl" was besieged by members of the press, radio, and television, and the coach limited her to about four interviews and photo sessions a month. Although gymnas-tics had never been very popular in America, Cathy's success brought wide attention to the sport and made her a celebrity. Thousands of young girls tried to emulate her, tying their hair back in pigtails and flocking to gyms all over the nation for acrobatic lessons. In one year she focused more attention on American gymnastics than the sport had received in its whole history.

Bud Marquette welcomed the exposure but did not permit Cathy to speak publicly unless he was present. Even then, the coach did most of the talking. Referring to her as his "peanut," Marquette would say, "I never had seen anyone like Cathy, and I guess I'll never find another one, either. She is the typical little American girl—a nice, clean kid . . . the American ideal . . . something like Shirley Temple. She's been very fortunate because she is photogenic and a pretty kid, but it hasn't affected her ego in any way. If it does, I'll just have to turn her over my knee."

Cathy commented, "He doesn't want me to grow up," but she worked on. In the months before the Olympics, Cathy's tensions and weariness showed in her performances. She was 19 years old and eager to quit gymnastics for a normal life. She found it difficult to concentrate during her routines and paid for these lapses in the form of injuries. At the National AAU Women's Gymnastic Championship in May 1972, Cathy was considered a certain winner. But on the final day of competition she lost her focus of attention for a split second, bruised herself seriously on the uneven bars, and had to bow out.

Cathy drove herself back to training. "People are expecting a lot from me," she explained, "and I don't want to let them down. They want a gold medal. So do I."

In spite of her poor showing in May, Cathy was chosen as a member of the American Olympic squad. She prepared for the Olympics with the single-mindedness and daring that had brought her so far. Her optional routine on the balance beam was twelve seconds slow, and she had to speed it up. So, 60 times a day she repeated the same series of moves, straining for steadiness, tightening, sharpening. Hands calloused from the bars and trembling with exhaustion, Cathy climbed up time after time.

Sometimes the frustrations couldn't be contained. "Once you think you've got your routines down, Bud starts finding things wrong with everything," she complained. Then, complaint over, Cathy went back to her routine. There was, she acknowledged, still much to do. "I have to work on my compulsories—a set routine everyone does—and I just have to be ready. I can't have any wiggles or wobbles or any kind of break in my routines."

Despite the fact that no U.S. gymnast had ever come close to reaching the level of the Russians or Europeans, Marquette predicted that Cathy would be a finalist at Munich. "She ought to place in the top three in balance beam, the top three in uneven bars, and the top six in all-around."

Cathy and Marquette had devised a unique back somersault on the beam, a move that was sure to impress the judges. Few gymnasts were fearless enough to attempt such a dangerous movement, one that might end their career in a moment. But Cathy, due to retire right after the Games, was going for broke.

For the uneven bar exercise, Cathy was planning a new dismount (the leap to the floor to finish a performance). This one, Marquette assured her, would become a modern standard and be named for her: "The Rigby Front." Added to that, the plan called for a one-and-a-half twist on the high bar, and a full pirouette on the low bar. She was to fly through the air, looking like a bird, and smiling, ever smiling.

Cathy was less confident about her floor exercises and vaulting. Her speed and low center of gravity wouldn't serve her too well there. The taller, more balletic gymnasts had the advantage in those events. So Marquette told her to make it through the vaulting as well as she could. And for the floor exercises, he chose such bouncy tunes for Cathy as "Beer Barrel Polka" and "Singing in the Rain." Most gymnasts worked to flowing, symphonic music. Cathy, however, needed a musical setting that would enhance, rather than detract from, her cute, muscular style.

Ready for the high point of her young life, Cathy and Marquette traveled to Munich in the summer of 1972, in the midst of a growing controversy. She was the only athlete allowed to bring her coach as a personal trainer, and this infuriated other American competitors. They called her a prima donna and a spoiled brat, and Cathy began to feel the stings of their hostility. "She is just too cutesy," some said, not aware that it was the coach and not the gymnast who wanted it that way. Hurt, Cathy withdrew from people, flashing the little-girl grin only when performing. While 1968 had been fun, this was deadly serious.

On the first day of competition, Cathy led the U.S. team in compulsory exercises. But it was all downhill from there. What Cathy faced, and what millions of American rooters had not been prepared for, was the number of utterly brilliant Russian and European competitors in the gymnastic events. While Cathy had been basking in the spotlight in the months preceding the games, these women had been carefully groomed with little fanfare. Delighted to have its first gymnastics star, the American public had put a terrible gold-medal pressure on Cathy. The truth was, the odds against her winning any medal were overwhelming.

The Russians had their own pixie, the totally unknown Olga Korbut, and she completely overshadowed the Californian. Cathy, suddenly cold with fear, faltered and slipped on the beam. This was the Olympics, and Marquette could not be out there in the arena, calming her, raging at officials when the scoring went against her, and pushing her on to more daring heights as he had always done.

With a brave, tremulous smile and tears glistening in her eyes, Cathy went through all her compulsories and optionals, but with no hope of winning. It *was* the year of the tiny, fearless girl gymnast, but it was Olga Korbut, not Cathy Rigby, who won the medals and the hearts of millions of viewers around the world.

As they had done for years, the Russians and East Germans completely dominated the women's gymnastic events. Cathy placed tenth overall. It was the best finish of any American—but it wasn't nearly good enough for Cathy or her fans.

The saddest thing was not that Cathy won no medals, but that the misinformed American public blamed her for losing. It was a cruel punishment to inflict on a young woman who had devoted her life to the sport.

After Munich, Marquette urged Cathy to continue her work, telling her that she could win in 1976. But Cathy was tired, emotionally and physically, and the magic spell had been broken. In January 1973, the 20-year-old married 33-year-old Tommy Mason and retired from gymnastic competition. She decided to go back to college and perhaps, some day in the future, open her own gymnastics school. As for Cathy Rigby, competitor—that chapter was finished.

When the deep disappointment of Munich was far enough in the past, Cathy looked back at her years of training. She saw the long path she had followed, a path of training and pain, of medals and injuries, the love-hate relationship with Bud Marquette, the fun she had missed and the sacrifices her family had made.

But she also remembered the excitement of competition, the many friends she had made, and the sheer joy of flying through the air. And if that wasn't enough to balance out the hardship, there was something else that told her it was all worthwhile. The sight of Cathy Rigby performing had sparked desire and ambition in thousands of young girls throughout America, who were now working hard to become strong and graceful athletes. Cathy had the immense satisfaction of knowing that she alone had made gymnastics an important part of the world of American sports.

The Cochran Sisters

SKIING

Gordon S. (Mickey) Cochran, a mechanical engineer, and his wife, Virginia, were self-confessed ski nuts. Every weekend in the late 1950s, from November to April, they longed to be out on the slopes. And it was a rare, unhappy day when they weren't. Living in Vermont, they had no trouble finding snow in season. But there *was* one hitch: the Cochrans had four small children. So . . . "because we didn't have money for baby-sitters," Ginny Cochran said, "we brought them along."

And that is how Marilyn (born in 1950), Barbara Ann (1951), Robert (1952), and Linda (1954) started skiing. It was all very natural and informal for the Cochran crew; just three little girls and a boy having fun in the snow.

Ski racing, the sport that was to become the center of their lives, began just as informally. "Our parents never forced us to ski," Barbara said years later. "Skiing was just something we did every weekend. When we were really young, we started skiing in the Lollipop races on Mt. Ascutney in southern Vermont. Everybody who finished the race got a lollipop."

By 1960, the large, active family had outgrown its small home, and the Cochrans started searching for a new place to live.

Skiing, which was already a mania for all of them, played a large part in their specifications. If they had run a newspaper ad, it might have read: *Wanted—sturdy rural dwelling for couple with four growing children. Must have many bedrooms and large, comfortable kitchen. Most important: property must include steep hill!*

After much hunting, the Cochrans found a large, old, two-story farmhouse at the foot of a very sharply pitched hill. The dream house was located in Richmond, a community of 1,200 people in northern Vermont.

By that time, the young Cochrans had developed into prize-winning skiers, accumulating trophies, mugs, and silver plates from local age-group competitions. These rewards were fine, but what mattered most was that they loved the sport and were eager to race, especially against one another.

"We were all very competitive," oldest sister Marilyn explained. "Until I was twelve or thirteen, I could beat my brother Bobby and a lot of the other boys, too. The first time Barbara beat me, I was flabbergasted. There has been a constant rivalry between us ever since."

Mickey Cochran, who had raced internationally in his own youth, had big plans for his children. With the help of the entire family, he cleared the hillside behind the new house and built a 400-foot rope tow, creating a ski course that the kids named Cochran Hill. The next step was the positioning of the slalom gates, pairs of poles topped with flags, scattered down the hillside at different intervals. A skier had to weave downhill in a zigzag pattern, passing through each set of gates in the proper order, or be disqualified. The winner was the one who covered the course in the shortest time.

Once the course was ready, the real work began. Cochran Hill became the personal training ground for the future Olympians. Winter and summer it was used by the kids. When there was enough snow on the ground (at least half the year in that part of Vermont), the hillside was an after-school and weekend practice slope. The youngsters loved skiing on their own mountain and never wanted to come indoors. Their father remembered, "I literally had to drag them off the hill at night."

In the summers, when even Vermont was bare of snow, the Cochrans continued to train. They would climb their hill and then dash back down through the slalom gates. There they'd be, in jeans or shorts, holding ski poles just as if they were on snow, darting down the grassy slope.

The Cochrans were a happy, tight-knit family. While other brothers and sisters were fighting and squabbling with each other, Marilyn, Barbara, Bobby, and Linda were out competing on the slopes. In their case, the normal rivalry that exists in every large family found a perfect outlet.

Mickey had definitely encouraged his son and daughters to participate in the sport, but they were the ones who decided to race. "When we started," Mickey Cochran said, "I just wanted them to have a ball going through the gates, without any pressure to win." He also made it clear to them that if they didn't enjoy themselves, they could forget about skiing in a hurry.

The young Cochrans were eager to pursue their sport, so Mickey devised a training program to go with the actual skiing. They started with basic calisthenics—push-ups and knee-bends. Then they added weight lifting to the program, using a 20-pound bar. When the kids mastered those exercises, their father had them try sit-ups (50 at a time) while holding a twelve-pound weight. The young Cochrans moaned and groaned about the workouts, but even in this they competed to see who could do it all faster and better.

The only part of their routine that caused any conflict was the long running sessions which Mr. Cochran started to keep them in shape during the summer. "Sometimes I can't get up to do it," Marilyn explained, "and Daddy gets very angry and we have a few heated words."

Barbara described her big sister as having a very quick temper. "Marilyn takes after Daddy," she said. "I love to run. I used to run home from grade school. That was about a mile. But I don't like working out with weights, though I never complain much."

Although they sometimes grumbled about their training, the Cochrans really enjoyed the family workouts. The same couldn't be said of their non-skiing friends, however. One teenage girl who visited the Cochran home came away horrified. As the girl's mother later explained, "She went to Richmond to spend a few days with them—a little vacation, she thought. She came home early. 'My God, Mother,' she told me, 'that place is a training camp. We were up at six to cycle for 20 miles, then play tennis, then run some more miles, then lift weights all afternoon. That's what they do for fun—lift weights! I had to come home to get some rest.' "

The Cochrans' world—skiing and training, training and skiing—was difficult for most others to understand. It set them apart from most non-Cochrans but drew them closer together. Still, they often thought about their lives, and about the things they were missing. Barbara once said, "I don't know what it would have been like if I had never ski-raced in my life. Sometimes I wonder what it would have been like to live a normal life. People in our hometown envy me, but they don't know that I envy them, too. They can do a lot of things I can't do. But then, I do a lot of things they can't do. It evens out."

Marilyn took a somewhat more positive attitude toward the situation. "I think we are getting more out of life," she said. "The kids at school are in their own little world."

Although the sisters were each other's best friends, Marilyn, Barbara, and little Linda also pointed out that they didn't really live in isolation. Like other dedicated athletes, they were part of a group. Their group consisted of about 20 skiers who met every weekend to race at Madonna Mountain in Jefersonville, Vermont. Nevertheless, it was still primarily a family affair, just enlarged to include others. "We would train while Daddy was setting up a slalom course, and we loved to run slalom," Barbara said, remembering those Madonna Mountain trips. "We were with the whole group we had grown up with, and skiing was something we did without thinking about it."

While her older and more proficient sisters raced in their age group, Linda raced in hers. Wearing baggy pants and rubber boots, and skiing without poles, Lindy, as the family called her, had a very easygoing approach to racing. Still too young to keep pace with Marilyn and Barbara in the rugged workouts, she regarded the sport as all fun and games. She would sometimes stop during a race, talk to people, and take extra minutes to finish the course. She didn't care how long she took, because every finisher got a lollipop anyway.

In 1964, when Barbara was 13 years old, she won a slalom, beating her older sister Marilyn for the first time on a public slope and in a *real* race. It was quite an exciting moment for her. "After that race," Barbara said, "they interviewed me for a radio program. It was my first interview and I giggled all the time. I giggled so much that they couldn't use the tape."

Before long, Barbara was her sister's toughest rival. Every year at the Eastern Giant Slalom Championships, the question was the same: which Cochran would win, Marilyn or Barbara? When Barbara was 15, she edged out 16-year-old Marilyn by .16 of a second in the giant slalom. "You beat me!" Marilyn screamed out half in praise and half in fury. Barbara just grinned. Of course, the day before, Marilyn had been the winner, beating Barbara by 2.97 seconds in the regular slalom.

The Cochrans didn't restrict their wins to the Eastern ski circuit. They were all over the place, winning one race after another. In 1966 Marilyn (then 16 years old) won the National Junior Slalom and was third in the Downhill, while Barbara (15) won the Giant Slalom. Together or separately, they were the most exciting American skiers to come along in many years.

Their training, under father-coach Mickey, continued at home. But Cochran Hill had some added features now—batteries of lights for night skiing and a 1,200-foot rope tow to supplement the old, shorter one. Even when they were in the house, eating or relaxing, skiing was the main topic of conversation. Mickey loved to talk about the sport. He would stand in the middle of the living room, demonstrating the use of ski poles. "Out in front of your body, like this, not trailing behind," he would explain, waving the poles as he spoke.

Barbara, Marilyn and Lindy Cochran arrive at the U.S. training camp to prepare for the 1972 Winter Olympics.

Barbara goes through a slalom gate on her way to a first-place finish in a 1971 World Cup race (top left), and Marilyn competes in a downhill event (bottom left). Below, Barbara gets a celebration ride on the shoulders of brother Bobby and teammate Rick Chaffee after winning a gold medal in the 1972 Olympics.

And, except for the days when the young Cochrans had too much homework, they'd be outside practicing. "We work out every night during the week," Barbara said, "and on Tuesdays and Thursdays other junior racers come over and we practice running slaloms. Nobody is compelling us to stick to the tough training life. We do it because we want to, and because we know that if you want something real bad, then you have to work to get it."

Mickey designed slalom courses, established training programs, and corrected flaws in his daughters' skiing. But he never tried to change their styles, which were very individual. Marilyn, standing 5-foot-7½ and weighing between 130 and 150 pounds, flailed away, arms flying, driving off every turn. Barbara, barely 5-foot-1 and weighing about 110 pounds, seemed to scoot through the slalom gates with no visible effort. Lindy's style was still not totally developed, but because she was close to Marilyn in height and weight, her technique was similar.

Over and over, Mickey would tell the girls to stick to their own styles and to go at the pace they felt was best for them. "This is the thing that matters," he would say. "You've got to know yourself." Speed and victories would come with work; what really mattered, he told them, was desire. "It's the same in any sport—football, baseball, for that matter, anything—life. Desire may not take you all the way, but it's the main thing."

None of the Cochran sisters made the U.S. Olympic team in 1968, which did not upset them or their father very much. In fact, Mickey Cochran had feared that they might be pushed too fast by circumstances and find themselves in world competition before they were ready for it. Mickey knew that his daughters needed more experience in racing and more maturity, and only time would bring those qualities.

Marilyn, who was then 18 and a senior in high school, would often end a losing race in tears, sobbing over her performance, unable to deal with the emotional tensions of heavy competition. She also had a weight problem, which affected her timing. If she did poorly in a race, she'd eat compulsively, sending her weight up to 150, which hurt her skiing. Then she'd diet, sometimes down to 120 pounds, and get so weak that she couldn't ski a demanding course without extreme fatigue.

Marilyn had, by her own admission, been outclassed in the Olympic trials. It wasn't that she had been lacking in skill, but in will. Still ruled by her emotions, she had lost to cooler, more mature skiers. This realization shook her, and she vowed to be more disciplined in the future.

At 16, Barbara was just too young and physically immature for the Olympics, and 14-year-old Lindy was even farther away from serious consideration. That was fine with Mickey Cochran; he was sure they would all be champions some day, so there was no reason to rush.

The years between the 1968 and '72 Olympics were good ones for the Vermont sisters, who filled them with a string of successes. In the U.S. Challenge races in March 1968, Marilyn went up against the same skiers who had beaten her in the Olympic Trials. But this time she was in complete control during the two winding plunges that made up the Giant Slalom. In an event that is often decided by a few hundredths of a second, she finished a whopping 2.42 seconds ahead of her second-place rival. It was a perfect exhibition of racing form, and one that led a noted ski coach to say, "That girl is fast! The truth is that lots of our collegiate men think they have good runs in practice if they can beat Marilyn's time. I personally think she can beat 90 percent of them."

Marilyn went from victory to victory. On a European tour in the winter of 1968–69, she won the Giant Slalom in Austria and placed second in two World Cup events in Czechoslovakia and Italy. In skiing, the World Cup is even more significant than the Olympics as a measure of a racer's ability. A skier who has one really good day can take home an Olympic medal; but to win the coveted Cup, she must do well all year long, competing in a large number of races held on different slopes all over the world. Competition takes place under all kinds of conditions, and again and again against the same rivals. To do well, a racer must have top-notch skiing ability, concentration, and most important, consistency. Marilyn had them all.

Barbara, Marilyn's toughest U.S. competitor, was not far behind her older sister. In 1969 Barbara took the U.S. National Giant Slalom Championship, running a superb race for her first major win. She was in total control all the way, streaking deftly down the well-packed snow of the twisting course.

Marilyn, who had come in third that day, was both happy for her sister and philosophical about losing to her. "She's another good racer I have to beat to win," Marilyn explained candidly. "When we're in a race, I just don't think of her as my sister. Of course, I'd like her to do well; but when she wins, that means I don't."

Marilyn paused, then continued, "I simply can't accept even a second- or third-place finish in a ski race. Sometimes I've said some things to her I wish I hadn't, because she did better. But we always talk it out later."

Barbara seemed to understand her sister's feelings perfectly. "I know Marilyn doesn't like it when I win," she said. "We pull for each other, of course, but mostly for ourselves. Actually, it's nice to have a brother and sisters around at a big race."

But the pressures were great, and there wasn't much the Cochran sisters could do but accept them. Obviously, if one of them won, the other had to lose. Even Linda, the youngest member of the "Flying Cochrans," was getting into the act. A quickly improving 15-year-old when Barbara won the '69 Giant Slalom, Linda had also been an entrant. She was disqualified for missing a gate, but the form and style were evident. It was just a matter of time before she, too, would be a serious rival. She was through skiing for lollipops.

Meanwhile, Marilyn and Barbara kept capturing the honors. At the 1970 World Championships, Barbara was second in the Special Slalom and Marilyn was third overall. Then in 1971, Marilyn became the first American—in fact, the first foreigner— ever to win the French championships. At about the same time, Barbara won two World Cup races.

The 1972 Olympics, to be held in Sapporo, Japan, were approaching, and America was pinning all its hopes on the Cochrans. In 1968 the U.S. team had been totally wiped out, much to the dismay of America's ski fans.

At the U.S Olympic Trials, Marilyn, Barbara, and brother Bobby qualified for the 14-member team; only 18-year-old Lindy missed out. Marilyn—then ranked fourth in the world in slalom, sixth in giant slalom, and eighth in downhill—watched her "baby sister" and commented, "Lindy's still so young, and it just isn't fair to saddle her with all the pressure she's had. All this talk about four members of the same family in the Olympics hasn't been good for her. But in the long run, she'll probably be better than any of us."

Marilyn, now a mature 22-year-old, was equally objective about her own skiing. "I'd like to do well in the World Cup and the Olympics," she said, "but I'm not going to condemn myself for the rest of my life if I happen not to be the world's best at something."

The weather was sheer misery at Sapporo in February 1972—even for winter-loving skiers. The slalom course, a tricky one under the *best* conditions, was made doubly treacherous by sudden snowstorms that swept some parts of the mountain and by fog banks that covered others. It was impossible for a skier to see more than one or two gates ahead, so everything depended on pure instinct.

Forty-two women competed in the special slalom. The winner would be the skier who had the fastest combined time for two runs. On the first course, 22 women were wiped out, including Marilyn, who fell at one of the early gates. Through all the skiing events it had been that way—falls, missed gates, slow times—and it looked as if the U.S. squad would again come home empty-handed.

Barbara Cochran had survived the first run, but her chances for a medal seemed slim. On the second course, she was the 15th to start. By the time the first 14 starters had finished their runs, the course would be slick and rutted, making Barbara's task even more difficult. "I didn't want to worry too much about it," she said. "So I decided that I would do my best, and even if I fell I would have that first good run to remember."

Out of the competition herself, Marilyn was there, encouraging her sister before the start of the second run. Then, in a pelting snowstorm, Barbara gritted her teeth and blasted through the starting gate. Snake-hipping through the 62 gates, she gathered speed, speed, and more speed. In and out of the fog she flew, her skis etching a smooth series of curls and curves down the steep mountainside.

When Barbara streaked through the finish gate she was surrounded by an eerie silence. Then her time was flashed on the electronic scoreboard, and a roar went up. She had won, with an overall time of 1 minute, 31.24 seconds. That was a scant two one-hundredths of a second faster than the next best skier, but it made all the difference in the world. Not since Andrea Mead Lawrence triumphed in the 1952 Olympics had any American skier—male or female—brought home an Olympic gold medal.

The years after the Olympics saw all four Cochrans skiing at the same level. Linda had finally caught up with her older sisters, and she began giving them some tough competition. Then in September 1974, Barbara announced she would not be competing that season. Instead she would spend her time guiding other young hopefuls as the women's alpine ski coach at the University of Vermont. Meanwhile, the other Cochrans continued competing, rooting for each other, training hard, winning some races, losing others—always thinking about each other's welfare even as they skied on and on toward the next World Cup, the next Olympics.

Micki King

DIVING

The spectators ringing the pool at the 1968 Olympics in Mexico City watched the American girl adjust the wheel of the 3-meter springboard. There were two dives remaining for each competitor, and Micki King of the United States was in the lead. Thoughtfully, she bounced on her toes, testing the springiness of the aluminum board that extended almost ten feet above the water. Satisfied, she turned and measured her steps back to her starting point. Micki smoothed back her short blonde hair and then she stood, expressionless, hands at her sides, thinking out every movement of the dive. One bad mistake and her score would drop, and someone else would win the gold medal in springboard diving.

"My last dive is always my bread-and-butter dive," Micki said, "so I felt that if I could be at least tied for the lead going into the last one, I'd win it. I knew that next-to-last dive, a reverse one-and-a-half layout, was the crucial dive. I've won meets on it, but it's very easy to miss. When I climbed up on the board I was nervous, but in a positive way."

The silence was electric as the judges and spectators at the pool waited. Micki pictured the way it would be: slow, graceful steps to the end of the board, the spring into the air, and the arrow-straight body turning backward one and a half times before knifing into the water, fingertips first. Micki had practiced the dive over and over for months and knew she had it cold. Everything was planned—the approach, the takeoff, the height she would reach before starting to rotate her body back toward the board, the point at which she would turn from head-up to head-down, and the precise place where her fingertips would enter the water.

"Supposedly," Micki said, "you work out enough to perfect it. But this time, when I went off the board, I knew it was far too fast. I knew I would rotate too fast. I had to adjust in the air to keep from missing the dive completely. In order to slow the dive down I had to put my arms in the air early, to elongate myself and to slow the rotation."

In a split second, Micki reacted to save the dive, extending her arms as a bird spreads its wings to catch the air. But while she was concentrating on that, she was coming perilously close to the board. Suddenly she felt a slash of pain in her left forearm. She had hit the board!

"The thud was so loud it echoed through the whole building," Micki said later. "I don't see how anyone could have kept from hearing it. I can still hear it now, and it makes me sick."

Miraculously, Micki didn't pass out from the pain. She continued the dive and entered the water plumb-straight. "I decided to fake-it-make-it," she said. "When I landed in the water I knew I was hurt. I felt very faint and I went into a mild form of shock. But I tried to act like everything was okay."

The seven judges, only two of whom were aware that Micki had hit the board, held up their scores. It was an unusually wide range—from $4\frac{1}{2}$ to 7 points on a scale of 10—and it was unusually low for a championship dive. It dropped Micki to second place, with one dive to go.

While the judges were holding up their scorecards, Micki was being helped from the pool by her frightened coach, Dick Kimball, who realized exactly what had happened. He took her behind a curtain, where a trainer held smelling salts to her nose and applied ice to her forearm to stop the bleeding. She had only ten minutes before her final dive, and Micki was trembling in a cold sweat, gulping air, green-faced and dazed. She tried not to think about the throbbing of her arm. Instead, she forced her mind to focus on her last dive—an even more difficult one-and-a-half reverse with one and a half twists. Again, she would have to leave the board facing the pool, rise in the air, and then rotate her body backward toward that menacing board one and a half times, while spinning one and a half times, so that she would cleave the water fingertips first, with her back to the board.

Another competitor might have dropped out of the competition, and no one would have criticized, but Micki never thought of scratching her last dive. The gold medal was now out of reach, but she knew that she still had a chance to take home a silver or bronze.

Micki went back to the board, using her good arm to turn the adjustment wheel that gave the board the proper amount of tension. Then she moved into her approach for the "bread-and-butter" dive, and sprang into the air. It took an effort of sheer will to move her throbbing left arm; yet Micki went through the motions, bringing her arms up together, lifting her body, turning, twisting, whipping her arms in close to her body, and snapping them out to a "T." But it was an agony of fiery arrows to move at all. She did it—every part of the dive—only it was a crude imitation of her championship style. There would be no medal at all for Micki, who finished the competition in fourth place.

"My immediate reaction was anger at myself for blowing it," Micki recalled. "The disappointment didn't hit me until the next day, when I saw the American flag go up at one of the other presentation ceremonies."

By that time, Micki knew she had broken the ulna, one of the two bones in the forearm. When she had gone to the U.S. team doctor after the competition was over, he had been furious to learn that she had gone on for that last dive. He raged about the permanent injury she could have done to herself, the danger to her arm, and to her heart because of the shock. But Micki hardly listened—she was too disappointed to care.

Her fans and the press, however, didn't know what had really happened. To them, Micki was a failure, a diver who had choked in top competition. The first news stories out of Mexico City accused her of falling apart in the clutch, and it wasn't until late the next day, when Micki appeared in a cast, that anyone understood the reason for those last disastrous dives.

The 24-year-old diver went home to the United States feeling that it was all over; she would never compete again. "I'd been training since 1960," she said bitterly, "and I'd done that dive a thousand times. The anger I felt at myself was greater than the pain of a broken arm. Instead of a gold medal, I won a plaster cast." After 14 years of single-minded dedication to her sport, Micki King announced her retirement.

Maxine Joyce King had been at home in the water almost from the day she was born on July 26, 1944. Her parents were outdoors people, and her father, an engineer in Pontiac, Michigan, encouraged Micki, as she was nicknamed very early, to swim when she was only a toddler. The Kings spent much of their leisure time at nearby lakes, where Micki happily learned her water skills. When she was four years old, her greatest joy was to have her father stand in the water and toss her into the air so she could somersault into a dive. Over and over, the little girl would clamber onto her father's shoulders to be thrown higher, farther.

Out of the water, Micki spent her after-school hours with neighborhood boys in their games. The Kings were pleased that their sturdy, intelligent youngster was so active, but they knew that when the boys were ready to join the many school teams open to them, Micki would be left with nothing. Therefore, Micki was encouraged to find a sport of her own.

Because the Kings lived in a cold climate, Micki's mother enrolled her in figure-skating classes. But even though her extraordinary sense of balance made Micki a natural on the ice, she hated the sport. "I tried it for a while," she said, "but I didn't like the routine. I still can't understand why I got bored with the routines of figure skating but not with those of diving."

When Micki was ten years old, she joined the local YMCA, which had an indoor swimming pool, and it was there that she saw her first diving board. Trying it out and finding that the spring under her feet gave her the same feeling she had had jumping from her father's shoulders, Micki announced that she had found her sport.

There was a great deal to learn about diving, and Micki started to absorb some of the techniques. During each session at the pool, she worked on the slow, steady approach—four measured steps that brought her to the end of the board, then the coordinated motions of the hurdle, and the upward movement of the knee preceding the downward foot-thrust that powered her into her takeoff. Repeatedly, she would go through the motions—four steps, arms straight down, then back like twin pendulums, quickly up into a "Y" position, then one leg up with toes pointed, arms back and down, foot down. Finally, arms up and one firm bounce on the board and off into space, flying toward the water.

Micki learned to dive for pure pleasure, with no thought of medals or trophies. She also enjoyed the small, special world of the divers. All the children worked at the sport together, watching and commenting on each other's dives, demonstrating bits of technique, talking of tucks (head and knees are brought to the chest, body is in a tight ball), pikes (arms and legs are straight, body is bent at the hips in a jackknife position), "sommys" (somersaults), and layouts. Each new dive was a trick to be mastered for the sheer joy and excitement of doing something well.

Watching her progress, her coach knew that the fearless youngster would soon be ready for competition. When Micki was 14, he took her from the low, 1-meter (3 feet, 3 inches) board on which the novice divers worked, and introduced her to the 3-meter (9 feet, 10 inches) board and the 10-meter (32 feet, 10 inches) platform.

That was the crucial testing point in Micki's early career: would she be able to put herself through the complex mechanics of her dives despite the terrifying heights of the takeoff? A diver is expected to have more maneuvers in a dive from the 3-meter level than from the 1-meter level. Neither Micki nor her coach knew how she would face these physical and psychological barriers, but she was willing to try.

First, the 3-meter board. Success—and Micki loved it. With the additional height enabling her to stay airborne longer, she would soon be doing all the intricate rotations and twists that had been impossible from the lower board.

Then she tried the platform, which provided no spring at all. To Micki, the high tower seemed to be "thirty-three feet up and a hundred feet down." Without a moving springboard, Micki had to supply the necessary height and momentum with her own body. She learned to accentuate the pendulum motion of her arms in the approach, building up the force that would, with her leg-bend and stretch, thrust her forward and up, arching into space, to begin her free descent.

When she was 15 years old, Micki entered her first formal diving meet. She never forgot it. "For the first time," she said, "there was a purpose besides doing a trick the boys couldn't do. Just as important, there was a trip. It was only a 90-minute drive to Toledo, Ohio, but we took off with all the excitement of a long voyage."

The Toledo YMCA meet was an eye-opener to the Michigan girl. "I had never seen any girl divers before," Micki said. "I won, but I wasn't cocky because I knew I had a lot to learn. I didn't even know the names of the dives I did."

Micki went on a regular training schedule of three sessions a week with the coach, trying to perfect the more complicated dives she needed to be a big winner. Divers are judged by two factors. The first is how well a given dive is performed. This is measured by the judges on a scale of 1 through 10 (the better the dive, the higher the score). The second is how difficult a given dive is to perform. The degree of difficulty (D.D.) is assigned to each dive and ranges from 1.2 for the easiest to 3.0 for the hardest.

A diver's score for a single dive is based on both factors. For example, if the seven judges in a major meet score the dive 6, 7, 7, 7.5, 7.5, 8, 8.5, the highest and lowest marks are disregarded and the other five are added together, giving a total of 37. That sum is then multiplied by the degree of difficulty. If the D.D. is 2.5, the diver's score for the dive will be 37 x 2.5, or 92.5.

It soon became clear to Micki that even if she performed perfectly on dives with a low D.D., she could still be beaten by divers who did more difficult dives. She realized that there was only one way to be sure of winning—master the hardest possible dives.

Micki was 16 years old and had been diving seriously for just one year when the Olympic Trials were held in Detroit in 1960. Remarkably, the slim, blonde novice qualified for the trials. At first she was reluctant to go, afraid that she would embarrass herself in front of the judges. But Micki's coach convinced her to enter, if only for the experience. And even though she finished 29th in a field of 30, she gained some much-needed competitive experience and got her first glimpse of world-class diving.

In 1962 Micki graduated from high school in Pontiac and enrolled at the University of Michigan. She was still uncertain about her future and wanted to spend every moment at her sport. But, as her father repeatedly cautioned, "Diving isn't going to be forever."

Michigan had fine facilities for water sports, and an excellent diving coach, Dick Kimball, with whom she could work. At the same time, she could earn a college degree and prepare for a career after she was too old to compete athletically. Micki majored in journalism and minored in physical education, but her "major" major was diving.

For fun, Micki swam on the women's relay team. She also took up a new sport, water polo; as the goalie, it was her job to protect the net from shots made by the opposing team. Water polo is a tough game, fit only for good, strong swimmers who aren't afraid of mixing it with others. Micki was such a stand-out goalie that she was twice named All-America—and water polo wasn't even her top sport!

When Micki came to coach Kimball, she still had a lot to learn. "She wasn't very good at first," Kimball remembered, "but I knew she was a good athlete." She was tall (5-foot-7) and well built, weighing 130 lean and muscular pounds. Most significantly, she possessed a quality that cannot be taught but without which no diver can be great. "People are always asking me, 'How do you know where you are when you come out of a dive, so that you won't land on your back?' " Micki said. "Well, it's just a simple matter of kinesthetics. That's an awareness of where your body is in space."

Micki King relaxes
after a 1972 meet.

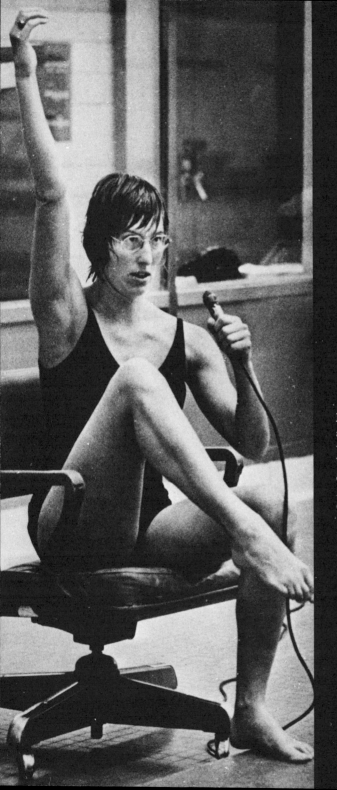

Micki uses the public
address system
while coaching the
U.S. Air Force Academy
diving team in 1974.
At the 1971 Pan Ameri
Games in Cali, Colombi
(right), she jack-
knifes high off the 10-
meter platform, seeming
miles above the pool.

With Kimball's coaching and encouragement, Micki went to work on the 10-meter platform. She had been up on diving towers before but had never done any really complex maneuvers. Now the 18-year-old college sophomore had to overcome her fear, pull together all the techniques she had learned, and hope that she would succeed.

It was a trembling Micki King who climbed the tower ladder again and again. "I would like to know what makes people jump," she said. "A lot don't at first, you know. They stand there on the edge and finally walk away. Height is the big psychological thing that scares people off. When you hit the water after jumping off the tower, you're going about 40 miles an hour. Sometimes you hit with such force that your shoulders and upper arms turn black-and-blue. I was scared for three years."

The courageous Micki was able to work within the normal human fear of falling from heights and compose beautiful dives. And because of her inborn kinesthetic sense, she never suffered the serious injuries that end the careers of many divers. There were bruises, of course, and the sting of occasionally hitting the water badly, but it was still fun. Frightening, but fun.

To supplement the water work, Dick Kimball had Micki do diver's gymnastics. "I do a lot of dry-land diving," Micki said. "We have a board secured to the floor and a foam-rubber pit similar to the pit a high-jumper lands in. I can practice my takeoff without getting wet and can have immediate correction. For instance, I'll do an approach and takeoff for a double front somersault and my coach will spot a mistake. Two seconds later I'll be back on the board trying that trick over again. We also train with the trampoline."

The trampoline exercises that Micki performed were not always the free-falling bouncing and turning practiced by gymnasts. Wearing a belt within a belt, Micki would be hoisted toward the ceiling on pulleys. With each side of the outer belt attached to the pulley rope, she could safely rotate forward or backward. The inner belt was filled with ball bearings which allowed her to twist and turn without becoming entangled in the ropes. Suspended in mid-air over the trampoline, Micki would work on spotting—picking out a visual point in the distance to gauge her height. Then, her kinesthetic sense telling her whether she was upside down or right side up during a rapid spin, she would piece together the twists and turns of her intricate dives. Only after Micki was certain of her tricks on land would she take off her safety harness and transfer the movements to the board or platform.

The constant practice paid off as Micki rose from 29th place in the 1960 Olympic Trials to 5th in 1964. She was then 20 years old, almost past the age of most world-class divers, but she was still improving. By the time she graduated from the University of Michigan in 1966, Micki had won three U.S. Nationals titles and the Canadian diving championship.

Micki didn't want to stop diving after graduation, but she was confronted with a problem that must be faced by all American amateur athletes—earning a living in a way that allows time for an all-consuming sport. Getting paid for anything connected with water sports—coaching other divers or even working with young swimmers—would have disqualified her from amateur competition.

Micki's parents had paid for her college education, but they couldn't afford to support her any longer. They also believed, as did Micki, that a grown woman should support herself. Micki looked around at the opportunities open to her and made a choice.

"I wanted to enter the Olympic Games in 1968," she said, "and I needed to fill the two years between graduation and the Games with training and also with responsible work. I wanted something different from the ordinary."

In the fall of 1966 Micki enlisted in the U.S. Air Force and entered Officer's Candidate School for training. "The Air Force was a chance to have a career and continue diving at the same time. This was something I couldn't find in civilian life," she said. Graduating from O.C.S. with a commission as a second lieutenant, Micki was sent back to the University of Michigan to work with the ROTC detachment. It was the ideal station for her, because she could continue to work with coach Kimball. By this time she was developing new dives to add to the diver's book. Micki was a true innovator, and she began to introduce combinations which had never before been done by any woman. Her back one-and-a-half somersault with two and a half twists and reverse one-and-a-half somersault with two and a half twists (this done from the 3-meter board) later became standard accepted dives.

With two more years of training, Micki and coach Kimball felt, she stood an excellent chance to take a gold at Mexico City. But then fate, in the form of a broken arm, stole the medal at almost the last second.

Micki returned to the United States with her arm in a cast and reported to a new Air Force assignment in Los Angeles. She wore the cast for almost four months, every day of which she spent wondering if she would ever dive again. When the cast came off, she couldn't even straighten her arm, and she was certain that her career was as shattered as the arm had been.

Resigned to a forced retirement from diving, Micki worked at the Los Angeles base, directing off-duty education programs for the Air Force. She commuted daily from her apartment in Hermosa Beach. Seeing her in uniform, her neighbors assumed she was a meter maid.

Micki enjoyed helping others, convincing dropouts to go back to school with military approval and funding. But her own life was at a standstill. Then in the spring of 1969 her life turned around once again.

"As fate would have it," she said, "the indoor Nationals were at Long Beach, only 23 miles from my apartment. I went as a spectator for the first time in eight years or so, and sitting and watching was the hardest thing I had ever done in my life. After that I talked to Dick Kimball, and he said, 'If you feel that way, maybe there's some diving left in you.' So I called the sports office at Randolph Air Force Base in Texas, and they said it was great that I wanted to dive again. They also said they would arrange for me to compete in the World Military Games in Pescara, Italy."

The trim, blonde lieutenant was then 25 years old, long past the age of retirement for most divers. She also was out of shape, but that didn't stop her. Working nights at a pool in Long Beach, doing special exercises to bring the strength back to her left arm, Micki began training for her comeback. In June 1969 she entered the Military Games, the first woman ever to compete directly with men in an international diving competition. After finishing fourth in springboard and third in platform, a proud and happy Micki said, "I was amazed at how quickly everything came back. I even had to learn two new dives that normally are done only by men."

Dick Kimball wasn't surprised in the least. When told of Micki's Military Games performance, he said flatly, "She dives like a man." To which another coach, whose divers had been edged out by the Michigan marvel, replied, "Hell, the men wish they could dive as well as Micki!"

In August 1969 Micki went on to the Santa Clara Invitational Meet in California, where she won both the springboard and platform events. It looked like clear sailing to the 1972 Olympics, but there were three years and many meets to go. One bad mistake, one serious injury, could end her dream.

The Air Force had so much confidence in their young officer that they gave her time off before each major competition so she could go back to Michigan to work with Kimball. Other divers, who didn't appreciate her grit, were less impressed. Dubbing her "Mother Max," they scoffed at Micki, saying the 25-year-old diver was too old to be a winner.

But Micki knew her sport, and she knew herself. "I don't feel I've yet reached my peak as a diver," she said coolly. "I started later than most girls, and I'm attaining my goals later. The fact is that in diving the thing you want most is consistency, and that comes only by repetition. In diving you can *always* get better. There are always new dives to learn and new styles to adopt. It requires years to perfect the mechanics and form and to attain that essential consistency."

Micki proved her point, taking medals in every meet she entered. Before the 1972 Olympics she won the Pan-American Games competition, the World Student Games, the International Invitationals, and a record-setting tenth U.S. Nationals title. There was only one more award she wanted—an Olympic gold medal.

In the summer of '72 Micki—now Captain King—went to the Olympics in Munich, hopeful but fearful. She couldn't erase the memory of that dreadful moment in 1968. "I never did try that dive again," she said. There were different tricks this time. Micki knew that each was as intricate and as risky as the one she wouldn't do; but she also knew that there could be no other way—"safe" divers don't win Olympic medals.

With her first effort—a forward two-and-a-half somersault—it was clear that 28-year-old Mother Max was the one to beat for the springboard title. Calmly, she climbed to the board for the rest of her dives, ran her fingers through her short, wet hair, and set herself for the approach. Four steps, the hurdle, and she was up, riding the air high above the board. Time seemed to stop as she hung in space before going into her quick, sure turns and plunging straight down into the pool. At times the water barely rippled as she broke through the surface. It was a display of pure grace, controlled power, and technique never seen before in amateur diving. By the end of the competition Micki had easily locked up her gold medal.

Then, and only then, was she satisfied. She had proven to the world that she was the greatest female diver, and to herself that she could break the grip of fear that had tormented her for four long years. She had done it all, and finally she was free—to sail boats, pilot a plane, relax and enjoy life. Yet she'd never be through with diving—it was too much a part of her life.

Early in 1973 Captain Micki King was named diving coach at the U.S. Air Force Academy in Colorado Springs, the first woman ever accepted as a faculty member of a military academy. She was also elected to the Governing Board of the U.S. Olympic Committee as an athletic representative.

The next phase of her life had begun: teaching others to whirl and tumble through space, effortlessly and fearlessly, helping them to overcome the heart-stopping terror of heights, molding them into beautiful air-borne athletes.

Micki also became an articulate spokeswoman for amateur sports, lobbying for aid and encouraging others to dream and compete. This was her crusade, and would be for years to come—to bring the delight and the discipline of sports to every youngster with a desire to learn.

Kathy Whitworth

GOLF

When her home town of Jal, New Mexico, celebrated Kathy Whitworth Day in 1965, Kathy recalled, "They handed me a picture of me. In it, I was standing in front of the house, and I must have been about two years old. I was holding this big old driver in my hand. I don't rightly remember doing that, but I do recall that when we played around as kids we'd drag a club and an old ball out of my grandfather's bag in the attic. We'd hit around like kids do with a stick and ball. I reckon we knew it was a club. But we didn't know it was golf."

In 1965 Kathy also was named Woman Athlete of the Year, and by this time she knew the game was golf—and everyone who knew golf knew the name of Kathy Whitworth. The tall, quiet young woman had been playing professional golf for seven years, and already she was recognized as one of the country's outstanding competitors.

Born in Monahans, Texas, on September 27, 1939, Kathy was the youngest of the Whitworths' three daughters. When she was still a baby, the family moved just across the state line to Jal, New Mexico (population approximately 5,000), where Kathy's father, Morris, bought a hardware store. It was a happy time for

Kathy, growing up in a friendly small town, attending Jal Public School, and playing in the wide open spaces.

An indifferent student in school, Kathy saved most of her energy for sports. "I played softball and football and wrestled with the boys," she said. "I could bounce them around. I was also good in basketball and other sports."

As Kathy grew up, however, she found fewer and fewer outlets for her fine athletic talents. Had she been born a boy, Kathy would have had no problem. She would have joined a baseball, football, or basketball team and probably become a neighborhood hero. Unfortunately, however, those sports were taboo for girls. It was all right to join the guys in a fun, pick-up game, but any girl who played seriously—which Kathy did—was ridiculed and rejected.

Sadly, the once bouncy, active youngster withdrew from others. She began to stay indoors after school and mope. Lonely and frustrated, she became a compulsive eater. Because she felt deprived of the thing she really craved—acceptance—Kathy spent all her time stuffing herself with food.

"I couldn't stay out of the refrigerator," she admitted. "My only sport was eating. I ate everything. I particularly liked chocolate milkshakes. My trouble was that I loved desserts. I was snacking all the time—and I ate pretty good when I sat down, too."

At first Kathy was only plump, but soon she became really fat. The Whitworths tried everything to get her to lose weight, but Kathy just wasn't able to control herself. Always taller than others her age, and different from most girls in her athleticism, she felt hopelessly unattractive. No diet would turn her into a soft, frilly creature, she reasoned, so why suffer when the result could never be satisfactory?

It was a vicious circle: feeling big and ugly, Kathy tried to comfort herself by eating—which naturally made her even heavier. By the time she was 13 years old, Kathy weighed 200 pounds. There was no physical or glandular reason—it was just a matter of too much food.

Kathy's mother, Dana, saw her youngest child hurt and bewildered and tried to find a solution to the problem. Words didn't seem to help; the more she nagged, the more Kathy ate. And Dana Whitworth worked with her husband in the hardware store, so she couldn't be home all day to supervise her daughter's eating habits.

Exercise seemed like one answer to the problem, so the big little girl went off to the tennis court to learn the game. Because she was quite strong, Kathy had no trouble hitting the ball well, but running was a chore. She was carrying around so much weight that she huffed and puffed with every stroke. Huge and ungainly, she felt like an elephant lumbering around while all the other players were gracefully darting and dashing. With tears in her eyes, Kathy saw the smirks of others at the tennis courts, and she went home.

Tennis, clearly, was not the answer. By the time Kathy was 14 years old and a freshman at Jal High School, her weight had gone up to 215 pounds. "I didn't weigh myself after that," she said, "but they say I ballooned up to 250."

The doctor warned her about the danger of obesity, the undue strain on the heart; her parents begged and nagged. But only Kathy had the power to do something about it. Then, in the spring of her freshman year, she finally decided to go on a diet. The other girls in her class were beginning to catch up to her in height, and Kathy realized that she could be a "normal-sized" human being if she just got rid of all that fat. The neighborhood boys were getting bigger, too, and Kathy, who was now 5-foot-7, no longer towered over them. She was maturing and, as she said, "I guessed how I'd like to look nice after all."

All that summer Kathy stuck to her diet, determined to start her sophomore year as a new, slimmer person. It wasn't easy, though. When she had nothing else to do, Kathy still ate too much. Then, one sweltering summer day, she made the great discovery of her life.

"Three friends of mine and I went out to the golf course," Kathy recalled. "I was shocked. I couldn't control that damned little ball. I was determined to master the thing. From then on, I was hooked."

To Kathy's surprise, golf was harder than it looked, and she was a girl who liked a challenge. More important, golf was an acceptable activity for a girl. Nobody could call her a tomboy for doing well on the golf course. And best of all, the game didn't require running, so a fat girl could play it without feeling foolish.

"I started playing every day," Kathy said. "It helped my diet, too. It got me out of the kitchen. Instead of sitting around the house, I was on the golf course—and away from the refrigerator. I was on the course *all day long*."

Outfitted with the proper equipment from her father's store, Kathy soon became a familiar figure at the Jal Country Club, where she chased that "damned little ball" day in and day out.

When school began again, Kathy sat through classes, her mind only half on her studies, waiting for the final bell to ring. Then, free at last, she'd hurry out to the club. There she would begin her real day.

For a while, Kathy progressed on her own, teaching herself to hit the ball farther and more accurately. But, although she improved steadily, she still needed help. She had been playing for about a year when she turned to Hardy Loudermilk, the pro at the Jal Country Club, for a few lessons. The big girl (she had reached her full height of 5-foot-9) was a "natural," but her self-taught stance was awkward and she tended to kill the ball with power when a gentler, more thoughtful stroke would have been more effective. The potential was there, but it was raw and untrained. Loudermilk worked to smooth it out.

Kathy's efforts were rewarded in more ways than one. Not only did her game improve—but so did her figure. One year on the golf course—and out of the kitchen—brought her weight down to 200. That was still more than she wanted to weigh, but having lost 50 pounds, Kathy knew that she could conquer her problem.

"I was quite proud of the fact that I *could* lose the weight," she explained. "I knew I looked better, and it made me feel better. It proved that if you made up your mind to do something, you could do it. Everything depends on your mental outlook toward life. If you have a defeatist attitude, it's bad. It's the same with a golf game. It's something you have to work on all the time."

By 1956, Kathy's junior year, Loudermilk was convinced that his student could be a champion, but that she needed coaching that he couldn't give. He suggested that the Whitworths take their daughter to Austin, Texas, and let Harvey Penick, a well-known golf pro and an excellent coach, have a look at her game. The Whitworths weren't poor, but they didn't have any money to throw around, and this would be a large expense. Yet, because golf had helped change their fat, unhappy child into a healthy-looking, confident teenager, they were willing to do everything possible to encourage her interest in the sport.

Loudermilk arranged an appointment for Kathy with Harvey Penick, and off she went with her mother. As soon as Penick saw the quiet, still-gawky 16-year-old play, he knew that with work she could be a sensation on the links. So for two years, as Kathy said, "Mother and I would ride the bus the 400 miles into Austin. We went a couple or three times during the summers. We could only stay four days at a time. Harvey would work every day with me from eight-thirty in the morning until five in the evening."

Then Kathy would go home to Jal and practice what she had learned, deeply motivated to succeed. Engrossed in her game, she dropped 25 more pounds during those years. After graduating from high school, Kathy entered her first big tournament, the New Mexico State Amateur. And to everyone's surprise, the young unknown won the tournament. Kathy was now the state champion.

With that victory adding confidence to her ability, Kathy pledged her life to golf. She enrolled in Odessa (Texas) Junior College but stayed only one semester. "They were supposed to be starting some new golf program," Kathy explained, "but it didn't work out. So Mom and Dad decided to put the money for my education to getting me some tournaments."

In 1958 Kathy entered the Titleholders Tournament in Augusta, Georgia. "I didn't play too great," she admitted, but she did get the feel of tournament competition and a chance to see some of the top golfers in action. Later that year Kathy repeated her New Mexico Amateur Championship triumph, but she was still too raw and unseasoned to do well against national competition. Kathy's inexperience was apparent in her next tournament, in Dallas.

"I was tied with another golfer for third-low in the amateurs," Kathy recalled with a smile. "We were told to go into a sudden-death playoff. Next thing we knew, a gallery had started lining up. No, not for us—Mickey Wright and Beverly Hansen were scheduled to go on. There must have been 4,000 to 5,000 people. I did about die! I hit my first straight up into the sky. I don't quite remember what happened from there except that my opponent got a par-four and I missed a four-foot putt. Even though I was embarrassed to death, it was sort of exciting."

Other golfers noticed Kathy, and were aware of her determination. Betsy Rawls, one of America's finest golfers, remarked, "Kathy and her mother came from Jal to Augusta by bus. Every day, they would get on a bus and ride it out to the course. Kathy really wanted to play."

She very definitely wanted to play, and her only chance for improvement lay in playing frequently against the best. The high cost of joining the competitive tour was a real problem, however, as the Whitworths could not afford to finance her much longer. Fortunately, others in Jal had faith in Kathy—and the money to back up their faith. Together with Hardy

Kathy Whitworth blasts her way out of a sand trap in the 1965 LGPA Midwest Open (left). Above, she winces after missing a putt in a 1968 Pro-Am tourney and jumps for joy after capturing the 1967 LGPA Championship.

Loudermilk and Morris Whitworth, two local businessmen agreed to stake Kathy. They would provide a total of $5,000 a year for three years so that Kathy could turn professional and join the golf tour. For her side of the bargain, Kathy would give them half of her earnings for those years.

Kathy applied for membership in the Ladies Professional Golf Association (LPGA) in December 1958 and launched her professional career early in '59. "I wasn't really ready for the pro tour," Kathy said, "but it would have been spinning my wheels for those three years otherwise. They were offering me the money which I couldn't take as an amateur."

It was hard going for the 19-year-old. After six lonely and frustrating months on the road, Kathy decided to go home. She hadn't won a thing, and she felt she was letting down her sponsors. "I thought I was going to be a bigwig," Kathy recalled. "I had been a big duck in a little pond. Now I was just a little duck in a big pond. There I was, shooting in the 90s. I hit my low ebb. I called Mom and Dad and said I wanted to come home. My family was very understanding. They suggested that since there were only two more tournaments before the tour would end for a two-week vacation, why didn't I stay out until then and see how I felt."

Kathy agreed to stick it out just a bit longer, and that decision proved to be a major turning point in her life. In Kathy's very next tournament, in Asheville, North Carolina, she tied for 15th place—and won a grand total of $71.25.

"Nothing else has thrilled me as much as that first check," Kathy revealed. "I felt so great. It had taken me so long, I didn't care whether it was ten cents. And I know that if I had gone home when I called my parents, I might never have gone back out. When you turn pro, your first goal is to get in the money. Your next goal is to get in the top fifteen, then top ten, then five. You are continually setting goals for yourself."

Kathy had high goals and, from that Asheville tournament on, she began her steady march toward achieving them. By the end of the year she had jumped from almost total obscurity to 26th ranking among professional women golfers. Her earnings that year were still small—$1,217—but Kathy was on her way.

It seemed that every day she showed another sign of improvement. Her weight was down to 160 pounds and she was beginning to develop poise. To Betsy Rawls, Kathy was "this wild creature from Jal, a big country girl who had no polish either as a person or a golfer. She just swung at the ball. As a result, she didn't develop as technically sound a swing as Mickey Wright or some others. Still, basically, Kathy is good at everything. Being so big and strong, she has a definite advantage even when she is not hitting her drives well. She gets the ball into position. It still goes straight and long. And the thing with Kathy is that she can improve her swing. I think she will definitely get even better than she is now."

Although she didn't win very much in her first few pro seasons, Kathy's golf improved noticeably. As her game got better, her weight dropped to 140 pounds, and she felt in control of herself off the course. This was important because it freed her mind for golf, and soon her new concentration began to pay off. In 1962 Kathy finished second to Mickey Wright in earnings, winning about $17,000. The following year she won $26,858. She was still second to Ms. Wright, but moving closer every week.

For a while, her sudden success seemed to throw Kathy, and she lost the silent concentration she needed to win. But she hadn't come this far to throw it all away. After one off-year, during which she earned only $10,435, Kathy got a grip on her game. Then, with Mickey Wright sidelined by a hand injury, Kathy had an open road to the top in 1965.

She went from tournament to tournament, piling up one victory after another. To prepare herself for each match, she would walk the course the day before play was to begin, analyzing it over and over in her mind. She checked the greens to see if they were running smooth. She studied the roughs, the approaches, the positions of traps. And she tried to anticipate any special problems that might be caused by weather conditions. With so much riding on each swing, every detail mattered.

Still, Kathy never agonized over each shot. She knew that mistakes are part of the game, and that thinking about the bad shot on the last hole could ruin her concentration on the next. It was intuitive playing: size up the situation, make up your mind, step up to the ball, and hit it. For a more nervous, intellectual golfer, it would never have worked. But that was the way calm, solid Kathy functioned, and that was the way she won.

Kathy knew her game—with its strengths and weaknesses—and stuck to it. "I don't hit the ball very far sometimes," she said, "but I can always steer it pretty good. Last year, when I wasn't hitting the ball so good, I learned how to think. When you're hitting the ball well, the tendency is not to think. I had thought that you had to hit the ball well all the time to win. But I began to look around and saw that there were girls winning tournaments who were not hitting well.

"The main thing is to get it in the hole, to play it the best way you can. I also began working on my putting and thinking over the putt. I was moving badly off my putt last year. I got to worrying so much about that, I forgot what I was out there for. So I changed my outlook, and that's the big difference. Now, before I get over the ball, I try to read the green. I try to keep my stroke as smooth as I can and keep it on a certain line. This is the mental picture I hold onto. I'm not hitting as many greens, but my chipping and putting are much better. I used to think that if you chipped one in, it was as if you stole it. I don't think that now. Just get the ball in the hole."

Kathy continued to get the ball in the hole, and in 1965 she won the first of her six Mickey Wright awards. This coveted annual prize goes to the woman who captures the most tour events of the year. Kathy also was named Woman Athlete of the Year in 1965 and '66. Each year her earnings rose, and by 1970 she had set an LPGA record with career winnings of $300,000.

Through it all, the fame and the financial success, Kathy continued to play her same steady game. Head down, addressing the ball, she would summon up every ounce of inner strength, tune out the entire world, and focus her entire being on the moment. The gallery of fans would wait in silence, not moving, lest they distract her in any way. Still totally absorbed, Kathy would take a deep breath, set herself firmly, and swing. Following through, she would watch the ball sailing through the air, straight and true. Then, a brief smile, and walk on.

Success didn't change Kathy's personality either. Quiet, thoughtful, and friendly, Kathy got along as well with the young players as with the stars. Her own childhood problems had made her sensitive to the problems of others. In a profession that has more than its share of jealousy and gossip, Kathy always stood apart from the squabbles. She could afford pretty clothes and a big car, and she had them; but she was careful not to flaunt her money and success in front of others.

Being a money-making golf star made the now slim and confident Kathy extremely attractive to many men, but she always felt that professional golf and marriage didn't mix well. "All of us feel quite liberated," Kathy said of herself and the other women on the tour. "We lead our own life, doing what we love. We don't have to worry about doing the dishes or cleaning the house, and it certainly beats the eight-to-five office routine. It would take quite a man to persuade me to give up this life. I'd be giving up too much."

Kathy invested her earnings and bought herself a home in Dallas, Texas, and a little beach house on South Padre Island, near Brownsville, Texas. But she never had much time to spend at either. She was always on the road. Kathy estimated that during any one year of the tour, she put about 40,000 miles on her car. She hated to fly and would drive to every tournament, spending long days and nights in the car, staying at motels near the golf courses on which she played. She was constantly packing and unpacking, hurriedly eating meals at roadside restaurants, attending to her duties as vice president and then as president of the LPGA, and, of course, playing golf.

There was never a moment to spare during the hectic tour season—but Kathy loved it. She described a typical tournament, starting with the Tuesday before play began: "First thing is to get clothes into the cleaner's and laundry. You are going to need them by Thursday or Friday at the latest, because we usually play in a pro-am [an exhibition match open to professionals and amateurs] on Thursday, and on Friday the tournament normally starts. Tuesday we also wash out our unmentionables, make hair appointments, and try to catch up on thank-you notes and letter-writing. If I feel like it Tuesday, I may go out and hit some balls to unwind. And if I haven't played the course before, I'll go out on Wednesday and try to get in at least one practice round.

"My being on the tournament committee means that every other week it's my duty to walk the course on Tuesday to check on water hazards, the general conditions of the grounds, etc., to see that it's in shape for tournament play."

Kathy generally spent her Wednesdays on tour hitting some practice rounds, then luxuriating at a beauty parlor, topping it off with a party or press interview in the evening. Thursday's pro-am play served as her practice round and gave Kathy her only opportunity to figure out the course by actually playing it.

"Once the tournament starts," Kathy explained, "I don't go out very much socially. From Thursday night on, I like to call my time my own. I want to relax, to think about the round I have to play. I don't want other things bugging me. Sometimes when a bunch of us are at the same motel, we get together to play hearts or some other card game, or go to a movie, or sit around and watch TV."

One year, when Kathy had a week off in California with nothing to do, she took up fishing. "I drove everyone along the way crazy," she recalled, laughing, "asking how do you do this, how do you put a fly on, how do you, how do you forever. It was a lot of fun. Sometimes it's nice to be just by yourself, too, to take stock of things. Not too often, though. I get kinda lonely."

Kathy was out there playing too often to ever get lonely for long. By the end of 1973 she had won countless major tournaments, earned a record-breaking total of $488,319, and been named LPGA Player of the Year seven times. Still the one to beat, though past 30, she said, "I'd like to play as long as I can. Someday I may get tired of it. But right now, as long as I can stand up and swing a stick, it's what I want.

"Some people say, 'But you're giving up a permanent place, security, family.' But then again, this is what I want to do. I have something just as good or better. For one, I'm my own boss. If I didn't like the game or want to be dedicated to it, then it would be a problem. A lot of people think professional golf is one big country club. It isn't, though it's still wonderful. I sometimes think the hardest part is trying to pack and unpack the car. But I just don't think we give up that much.

"People also say, 'You can't do anything but golf. And you have to go to all those parties.' But that all depends on how you look at it. Golf has given me the opportunity to travel, to meet new people, to make new friendships. Why, it has been worth every bit of it."

When the traveling just became too much, Kathy would finally retire from the circuit. But she didn't think about that very often. Golfdom's leading female money-winner lived for her game. It was the source of her inspiration and fame and happiness. She lived it and loved it so well because she never lost her fascination with that "damned little ball." And as she frequently reminded her friends, "If it wasn't for golf, I'd probably be the fat lady in the circus now."

Index